D1478516

Hans Jonas

Eric Voegelin Institute Series

in Political Philosophy

Hans Jonas

The Integrity
of Thinking

David J. Levy

University of Missouri Press Columbia and London

Copyright © 2002 by
The Curators of the University of Missouri
University of Missouri Press, Columbia, Missouri 65201
Printed and bound in the United States of America
All rights reserved
5 4 3 2 1   06 05 04 03 02

Library of Congress Cataloging-in-Publication Data

Levy, David J.
   Hans Jonas : the integrity of thinking / David J. Levy.
      p.   cm. — (Eric Voegelin Institute series in political philoso-
phy)
   Includes bibliographical references and index.
   ISBN 0-8262-1384-7 (alk. paper)
   1. Jonas, Hans, 1903–   1. Title.   II. Series.
   B3279.J664 L48   2002
   193—dc21   2001057464

∞™ This paper meets the requirements of the
American National Standard for Permanence of Paper
for Printed Library Materials, Z39.48, 1984.

Text design: Elizabeth K. Young
Jacket design: Jennifer Cropp
Typesetter: The Composing Room of Michigan, Inc.
Printer and binder: The Maple-Vail Book Manufacturing Group
Typefaces: Apollo, Carolina

Contents

Acknowledgments and Dedication *vii*

List of Abbreviations *ix*

1. A Thinker in His Time *1*

2. Gnosis, Reason, and the Challenge of Existence *11*

3. Organic Being and the Philosophy of Life *35*

4. Anthropology and the Identity of Man *62*

5. Ethics and Responsibility in a Technological Age *77*

6. Theological Perspectives *95*

7. Philosophy and the Future *132*

Index *143*

Acknowledgments and Dedication

I wish gratefully to acknowledge the generous support of the Earhart Foundation during the period of writing this book, which has emerged as part of a wider project, "The Hermeneutics of Order," as yet uncompleted.

The work itself is dedicated to my friends Jonathan and Teresa Sumption, without whom it would never have been written at all.

David J. Levy APRIL 2001

Abbreviations

GR   Hans Jonas. *The Gnostic Religion: The Message of the Alien God and the Beginnings of Christianity.* Boston: Beacon Press, 1963

IR   Hans Jonas. *The Imperative of Responsibility: In Search of an Ethics for the Technological Age.* Chicago: University of Chicago Press, 1984.

MM   Hans Jonas. *Mortality and Morality: A Search for the Good after Auschwitz.* Edited with an introduction by Lawrence Vogel. Evanston, Ill.: Northwestern University Press, 1996.

PE   Hans Jonas. *Philosophical Essays: From Ancient Creed to Technological Man.* Chicago: University of Chicago Press, 1980.

PL   Hans Jonas. *The Phenomenon of Life: Toward a Philosophical Biology.* New York: Harper and Row, 1963.

Hans Jonas

A Thinker in His Time

In 1974 Hans Jonas published a collection of his philosophical essays. The volume was subtitled "From Ancient Creed to Technological Man," which indicates the remarkable range of his thought. Jonas was not one of the best-known thinkers of the twentieth century, but he was, in my view, among the most important, and the significance of his work is likely to become more apparent in years to come as we seek to wrestle with the emerging problems of an age in which human agency has been extended to an unprecedented extent into areas formerly impervious to our will. In this brief book I hope to show why this is so and why the writings of this particular product of the German philosophical tradition have a relevance and a topicality that far transcends the circumstances of their origin.

In this first chapter I shall give a brief account of Jonas's life and of the circumstances in which his thought developed in response to the events of his time. In doing this I hope to show how a life's work, which began with a study of the problem of free will in St. Augustine and the study of ancient Gnosticism, came to encompass a philosophy of nature and a study of man's ethical responsibility as, in Heidegger's phrase, "the shepherd of Being" that provides a perspective on our present position and future prospects that is, in its power and wisdom, unequalled in the work of any of his better-known contemporaries. His philosophy is deserving of a much wider audience than it has thus far received.

This is a bold claim but not, I think, unjustified, given the sort of problems we face in a world in which the increasingly transformative power of human science and its concomitant technologies find no equivalent in the sphere of human wisdom in dealing with their potentially earth-shattering consequences. Jonas was primarily a philosopher, but the themes to which he was drawn by the logic of his reflection were of anything but purely academic import. In an age in which academic philosophy has, in large part, withdrawn from the great issues that move and excite the times, his work exemplifies the way in which an acutely honed philosophical mind can

1

clarify what is at stake in the decisions that we make and on which our future depends. Fortunately, and unlike many of his fellow philosophers, Jonas was a thinker who not only thought deeply but also wrote clearly in a style that is all the more remarkable because English was not his first language. Indeed, one notable feature of his works is a distinctive eloquence that make them as pleasurable as they are enlightening to read. That this should be true of a German-born thinker, and one taught by Martin Heidegger at that, is one of the most extraordinary things about Jonas's work. That this clarity should have been achieved without sacrificing the genuine complexity of the issues with which Jonas deals is a lasting reproach to the prevailing, overburdened academic jargons of our time.

The genial clarity of Jonas's prose is matched throughout by the exceptional integrity of his reflections. Integrity, here, should be taken in a double sense. On the one hand, his work conveys an enviable honesty of approach. Jonas never evades an issue by escaping into the sort of mystifying technicalities or pseudopoetic outbursts that mar the work of his first, great master, Heidegger; and, when his path leads him in directions that are purely hypothetical, he is at pains to indicate not only the speculative nature of his considerations but also the reasons why he believes such speculations to be both worthwhile and necessary in the face of the problems with which he must deal.

Like that of his great contemporary, Eric Voegelin, with whom he can be justly compared, Jonas's philosophy is anchored securely in a consummate mastery of the empirical material of which he tries to make sense. Like Voegelin, and unlike Heidegger, his is a philosophy that stands in continuity with scientific inquiry of which he takes full account in providing an intelligible account of the nature of man's being in the world. His work is never mystifying, and when, for example, he enters the field of theological inquiry, as he does in some of his late writings, he is careful to indicate of what the mystery of man's relationship to a world-transcendent deity may consist. Here he is frank in avowing the necessarily speculative nature of the answers he seeks to provide to the abiding questions of man's ultimate origins and destiny as a finite part and partner in the infinite process of creation, compelled, by the logic of rational inquiry itself, to search, recurrently, for ways of securing a meaningful existence for himself within a process that transcends him in space and time and so, at the limit, escapes the bounds of positive knowledge.

Unlike Voegelin, or Heidegger for that matter, Jonas does this without recourse to verbal neologisms that can leave the reader dazed and confused in a torrent of unfamiliar and sometimes needlessly unhelpful vocabulary. In comparison with other philosophers who have wrestled with related problems and mysteries, Jonas is an astonishingly clear guide who respects the integrity of a common tongue and his own recognizably right reason. In his philosophical discourse he is eccentric only in his avoidance of eccentricity. His work repays and often requires patient and intelligent attention but never demands a suspension of rationality or common sense. In this sense he is a profoundly worldly philosopher whose feet are firmly on the ground even when his mind is focused upon the stars.

The other sense in which the integrity of Jonas's thought stands out is the way in which his account of man's existence seeks to encompass the full variety of human experience in all its manifold modes. It is this encyclopedic ambition, authentically Aristotelian in its scope, that unifies his works, which range from his early studies of ancient myth and religion, through a philosophy of nature, to the studies of the place of ethics in an overwhelmingly technological age that crown his final years. This unity of rational inquiry is anchored in the circumstances of Jonas's life and the degree to which his thought arises as the sustained response of one highly articulate individual to the troubles of his age. Of Jonas it may be said, as Matthew Arnold said of his friend Arthur Hugh Clough, that "He saw life steadily and saw it whole," and, in an age of intellectual, moral, and spiritual entropy, this makes him an exemplary thinker for our time.

Hans Jonas was born to a German Jewish family in 1903 and, in his own words, was educationally "formed during the 1920s in the school of such teachers as Husserl, Heidegger and Bultmann" (*PE*, xi). His thematic debt to such thinkers and the phenomenological and existential currents they represent is apparent throughout his work, but, as I have suggested, while he follows their example in insisting on the concrete experiential sources of all authentic philosophical inquiry, he is mercifully free from their stylistic tendency to cloak such experience in a shroud of technical jargon impenetrable to all but those formed in their arcane schools. This makes him

an admirable ambassador for a current of thinking that is often regarded with suspicion by English-speaking critics who consequently miss the genuine content of its teaching and the degree to which,
in contrast to their own familiar analytic style, the masters of continental philosophy never lose touch with the ties that bind the
technical problems of philosophy to the urgent problems of life. In
Jonas's case it was the problems of a young German Jewish scholar
faced with the rise of Nazism that decisively influenced the direction of his thinking and led him toward the profoundly practical orientation that even his most theoretical work was to take.

Along with Karl Löwith, Hannah Arendt, Herbert Marcuse, and
Leo Strauss, Jonas was one of the gifted Jewish students who were
taught by Heidegger, under whom he took his doctorate at Marburg
in 1930. His first published work, on the problem of free will in St.
Augustine, appeared the same year, and the first volume of his study
of Gnosticism was published some four years later in a Germany from
which he had already emigrated in response to Hitler's attainment of
power. When, in 1933, the German Association for the Blind expelled its Jewish members, Jonas left his native land in disgust at
what, characteristically, he called the Nazis' "betrayal of the soli-
darity of a common fate."

From Germany Jonas made his way, via England, to the then
British protectorate of Palestine. On the outbreak of war, he enlisted in the Jewish Brigade of the British Eighth Army, refusing the
chance to work in military intelligence, in order to take part in the
physical struggle required to overcome Nazism. He fought in North
Africa and Italy before, in 1945, returning to Germany—thereby re-
deeming a promise made on emigration that he would never return
except as a member of a conquering army. In the meantime, while
on leave, he had married his wife, who, throughout the war, kept
him supplied with the books on biology that were to provide the
material out of which his work *The Phenomenon of Life: Toward a
Philosophical Biology* (1966) was to emerge. Like his determination
to take part in active fighting, Jonas's turn toward the philosophy of
the organism and its struggle for existence is evidence at once of the
integrity of his thought—his refusal of every temptation to isolate
thinking from living, mind from the matter in which it is embedded—and his recognition that each field of existence, the task of
theoretical reflection as well as the imperative of practical action, has

its own intrinsic imperative. One no more defeats a political evil without fighting than one makes sense of living being without studying its defining and distinctive processes. This Jonas clearly saw and acted on what he had seen.

In his introduction to his 1974 anthology of essays, Jonas speaks tellingly of the motivations of his work during the "five years of soldiering in the British Army" in which, "cut off from books and all the paraphernalia of research" he had to cease work on the study of Gnosticism. "The apocalyptic state of things, the threatening collapse of a world, the climactic crisis of civilization, the proximity of death, the stark nakedness to which all issues of life were stripped, all these were ground enough to take a new look at the very foundations of our being and to review the principles by which we guide our thinking on them. Thus, thrown back on my own resources, I was thrown back on the philosopher's basic duty and his native business—thinking. And, while living in tents and barracks, being on the move or in position, tending the guns or firing them, all the reductive primitivism and ordered waste of the soldier's life in a long war are most unfavourable to scholarly work, they do not prevent, are even preeminently conducive to thinking—and thinking to the point—when there is a will to it" (*PE,* xii). It was out of this experience, and the use he made of it, that the defining character of Jonas's postwar philosophy, its simultaneous concreteness and universality, was to emerge.

Terms—like "situated being," *Dasein,* or resolute decision—that in Heidegger himself and some of his students can seem abstract, impressionistic, or empty of ethical substance become, in Jonas's work, suffused with content and imbued with a directional sense that is always ordered to understanding the particular conditions in which the specifically human life form can flourish. It is true that Jonas's concept of existential thought owes much to Heidegger and that the ethical theory developed in *The Imperative of Responsibility: In Search of an Ethics for the Technological Age* (1984) can be seen as a modern reformulation of a Kantian morality of ends conceived, by way of a categorical imperative now extended beyond man to the continued being of nature, as good in themselves. Nevertheless, it is Jonas's anthropological orientation, toward the comprehension and furtherance of the good life, that leads me to think that Jonas's deepest philosophical affinities are with Aristotle.

Like Aristotle, Jonas is supremely attentive to the biological bedrock on which even the most apparently spiritual endeavors depend, and out of which they emerge as means of guiding and assuring the continuity of earthly existence. It is this focus that allows Jonas's philosophy to escape not only the Cartesian trap of supposing that mind and matter are ontologically distinct and incommensurate substances linked, if at all, by a mysterious bond impenetrable to reason, but also the potentially vacuous moralism that, in Kant, perceives obedience to duty as an end in itself. It is also this implicitly Aristotelian linkage of reason and right judgment with the innate imperatives of life itself that prevents Jonas from supposing, like certain other broadly ecologically oriented thinkers, that the only alternative, or supplement, to a purely technologically ordered rationality, based on attainment only of what we happen to be able to achieve, is to appeal to the blind force of intuition or instinct. These are points that must be developed further in later chapters. For the moment it is enough to note that, in Jonas's case, the motivation that impelled his thinking in such directions arose not from a reverent appropriation of ancient authorities, however admirable, but from his own rational response to his given fate.

On his return to Germany, Jonas renewed his contact with some of those he later called "the untainted few." Among these he mentions the theologian Rudolf Bultmann and the philosopher Karl Jaspers, who urged him to complete his study of Gnosticism; Jonas's first volume had, despite lack of any official recognition, received a surprising degree of eminence in scholarly circles since its publication eleven years before. But Jonas was not ready to return to that work; his second German volume was not to appear until 1954. Nevertheless, his reputation as a student of the subject was already made and an English summation of the two volumes, under the title *The Gnostic Religion: The Message of the Alien God and the Beginnings of Christianity,* was published, again to great critical acclaim, in 1958. Despite its apparently specialist nature, this is probably Jonas's best-known English work, not least because of the way Jonas was able to relate the strange, complex, and fearful world of Gnostic myth to the existential problems and anxieties of his own times. This again is a topic to which I shall return when I look at the way in which Jonas discovered in ancient Gnosis a clue to ultimately deficient, dualistic modes of thought that he identified, in renewed form, in the typical worldviews of modernity.

Despite the urging of former colleagues, Jonas chose in November 1945 to return to Palestine, where he met up once more with the wife he had last seen on leave in 1943. Less happily, he also discovered in Palestine that his mother had been murdered in Auschwitz—an experience which was to condition the theological perspective that he developed extensively only in essays written long after the event, and which were posthumously collected by Lawrence Vogel in *Mortality and Morality: A Search for the Good after Auschwitz* (1996). This volume contains, in addition to a substantial selection of Jonas's theological writings, a number of representative essays covering other aspects of his thinking, and, together with the editor's introduction, it serves as a useful single-volume introduction to the sum of Jonas's thought.

In Palestine Jonas joined, in 1948, the nascent Israeli army and served in the war that established the existence of the Jewish state. However, he did not settle in Israel but, in 1949, took up a fellowship at McGill University in Canada. In 1951 he was made assistant professor of philosophy at Carleton University in Ottawa, his first full-time academic appointment, and, in 1955, he succeeded Karl Löwith as professor of philosophy in the graduate faculty of the New School for Social Research in New York, where he remained until his death at the age of eighty-nine in 1993. These last were, not unnaturally, his most intellectually productive years.

In his latter years Jonas traveled widely, lecturing on the guiding themes of his work and gaining, especially in Germany, a broad audience that extended far beyond the academy. International conferences and seminars provided him with an opportunity to develop the implications of his ideas for policy makers concerned with the increasingly urgent problems raised, in so many fields, by the extension of technology. At the same time such forums allowed him a platform in which he was able to develop the far-reaching implications of both his philosophical anthropology and his moral, theological reflections for matters of public concern.

Jonas was on his way to one such gathering when I was able to speak with him in London in consequence of a brief appreciation of his work that I had written for the *Times Higher Education Supplement* and that he had happened to read. At this time the philosopher was well into his eighties, yet I found him a conversationalist of undiminished vigor; he was anxious, as much or more than ever, to bring his thinking to bear on the emerging problems of bioethics and the threatened state of the ecological balance that he perceived as the supremely important problem facing humanity in the closing years of the twentieth century. I had the impression that he regarded these problems as no less threatening than the political evils against which he had fought some forty years before, with the additional, complicating factor that the new threats were not the fruit of the penchant of the human species for committing evil deeds against their fellows but came from the pervasive thoughtlessness with which human beings were pursuing goals, apparently good in themselves, but fatally disturbing to the balance of nature on which the survival of the species continued to depend. I left our meeting with the impression of a physically small man endowed with a greatness of soul rare in his or any time and, returning to his writings, found myself more puzzled than ever that in Britain and America his ideas had not had the impact they deserved.

In Germany the case was different, for there his writings on technology, on the philosophy of nature, and on medical ethics circulated well beyond academic circles. There Jonas was a frequent participant in gatherings that brought together leaders of business, politicians, and academics, and, in particular, he is said to have had a considerable impact on the thinking of the Green Party in his native land. Certainly, I can testify that traveling in Germany I found editions of many of his books prominently displayed in station bookstores suggesting that, ironically perhaps, it was in the land of his birth that his ideas had achieved their greatest impact.

In some ways the pattern of Jonas's life repeats a story of exile in the face of the threat of death at the hands of a brutal ideologically inebriated regime that is all too familiar in the lives of twentieth-century thinkers. Much of the most remarkable work in philosophy, and in the human and natural sciences, in British and American universities over the last fifty years was accomplished by men and women who, had they stayed in their native lands, would have perished at the hands of their domestic enemies. Yet in Jonas's case, there was at least one unusual feature in that, unlike most of his fellow exiles, he chose to engage directly in the physical struggle by enlisting as a frontline soldier. I do not want to romanticize the soldier's life, nor to diminish the extent in which other ways of participating in the war for freedom contributed to the victory over the Axis powers, but at the same time I cannot help feeling that the role that Jonas chose reflects a directness of engagement that was typical of the man and his style of thought and that this directness is, in some ways, echoed even in the style of his theoretical and literary work. Reading Jonas, one is never at a loss to know against whom and what his work is directed. And this is a feature that is, if anything, magnified in the work of his later years in which his attention was turned specifically to the problem of man's future in a technological age.

Among the major thinkers of his time, only Jonas's first mentor, Martin Heidegger, devoted so much sustained attention to this matter, but, typically, Heidegger's thoughts on the issue—summed up in his remarkable and suggestive reading of technology as an extension of the metaphysical traditions formative of Western civilization—are, at once, more original and more obscure in their implications than those of Jonas. One cannot imagine Jonas ever saying, as Heidegger did in his late interview with *Der Spiegel,* that in the face of our predicament "Only a god can save us." Not only was Jonas only too well aware that any such expectation of divine intervention in the face of mortal peril was almost certain to be disappointed, but also his whole style of thinking, though influenced by Heideggerian existentialism, was much more trustful in the powers of human, practical reason to guide the future course of events. In contrast to Heidegger, Jonas believed in the continuing efficacy of Aristotelian practical reason—*praxis* as opposed to *techne*—as a countervailing power to the blind power of a potentially fatal technology; the great work of his final years, *The Imperative of Responsibility,* can, as I have suggested, be read, on one level at least, as an attempt to vindicate the Aristotelian conception of the necessity of renewing and cultivating just such a form of reasoning in the face of Heideggerian fatalism.

It is just this project, eminently practical in its implications for education, that makes Jonas, more than Heidegger, potentially the most potent philosophical guide in our future dealings with our ecological concerns. For what Jonas requires of us is not an attitude of passive expectation and hope but an active, rational engagement with the issues that we face, guided by capacities that we know to be part of the human equipment in the face of a world in which, in changing ways, human being has always been at risk. Jonas shares with Heidegger an appreciation of the extent that human prospects have been transformed in a potentially fatal direction by the dynamic of technological innovation over recent centuries, but he is very much more practical in his recommendation of remedies that are actually to hand. The extent of this practicality can only be shown when we turn to examine the argument of *The Imperative of Responsibility* in some detail later in this book, but for the moment it is enough to suggest that if Heidegger is the preeminent Cassandra or Jeremiah of the age to come—a prophetic voice who should not be ignored—then Jonas is the practical educator to whom we should look in our search for salvation from potential disaster as we attempt to regulate our simultaneously creative and destructive capacities to guide the future course of being. Perhaps only this can ensure our survival on a finite earth in which not everything that is technically possible is either desirable or conducive to survival.

Jonas's philosophy of practical reason and the ethical teachings that form an integral part of that philosophy are, perhaps, the crowning achievement of a life's work that, had circumstances been different, might have been devoted to more purely scholarly research in the area of the existential history of religion. As it is, the pressure of events formed and refined a body of thought of much broader significance for all mankind. If Kant can be considered the preeminent moral philosopher for an individualized bourgeois world, Jonas may just be an equivalent figure of equal significance for an age of technologically conditioned globalization from whom we must learn if right is to continue to be done and the integrity of man and earth preserved for generations yet to come.

That, at least, is the conjecture that guides the present book and leads me to hope that it will direct more people to an appreciation of a twentieth-century master whose time is still to come. But for that to occur, we must first understand the unified logic of informed concern that links the apparently diverse areas of Jonas's philosophical work. To that end I shall now examine, in broadly chronological sequence, the various writings of which that work consists.

Gnosis, Reason, and the
Challenge of Existence

✳

Taken in themselves, Hans Jonas's two-volume German-language study of Gnosticism and his English publication, *The Gnostic Religion,* would ensure his place among the foremost philosophers and historians of religion. Gnosticism itself, as we shall see, is a significant spiritual phenomenon in its own right. Knowing something about its ancient form helps us to understand the Christian identity and historical formation of our ancestral civilization; it is also a representative existential stance that is, in some sense, permanently available to human beings struggling to make sense of their existence in an always puzzling and often threatening cosmos. Nearly fifty years after its publication, *The Gnostic Religion* remains the best synoptic survey of the extraordinary variety of doctrines and myths of which gnostic teaching consists; and, at the same time, no one can read Jonas's account without being struck by how far elements of that strange and exotic teaching prefigure attitudes to the world that still prevail today, albeit in undoubtedly novel forms.

Since our subject is not the history of religions but the significance of Hans Jonas as a thinker for our time, our discussion of his account of the content of Gnostic teachings will be confined to those issues that bear upon the elements within it that he sees as relevant to his understanding of the contemporary world. This means that we must set aside much of the fascinating mythical material contained in his book and look, above all, at the structure of Gnosis and, by implication, its anthropological import. In other words, we do not seek to summarize what is itself a compendium of scholarly research in the study of the manifold Gnostic sects, but to examine the ways in which such apparently strange doctrines, many of them quite fantastical in their concrete mythological complexity, were able to provide answers to dilemmas forced upon human minds essentially no different to our own.

Given that there are today some who seek to deny that there is such a thing as an essentially unchanging human nature, and others, again, who make the less bold claim that what endures of that

nature in history is less significant than what changes, the idea that
there is in ancient Gnosis a model of meaning relevant to and comprehensible to modern men and women will seem itself to beg the
question of whether there is, in fact, a lasting human essence to
which both ancient Gnosis and an intrinsically nihilistic modern
philosophy can be said to respond. Jonas has an answer to such skep-
tics, and it is, in the way it is formulated, especially in his essay
"Change and Permanence: On the Possibility of Understanding History," the most convincing answer that I know. However, it would
be wrong to introduce it at this point because to do so would be to
distort the biographical logic of Jonas's own thought, which begins
with his inquiry into the phenomenon of gnosticism and, only then,
by way of the structural parallels that he finds between ancient Gnosis and modern metaphysical and ethical nihilism, proceeds to the
development of an anthropological theory in which rational affir-
mation of the constancy of man's innate nature and his worldly condition play a pivotal role.

Thus, though it is tempting to take the shortcut to Jonas's mature
philosophical anthropology, to do so would be to ignore the way in
which Jonas's own research in apparently exotic ancient religious
doctrines led him to a position in which he was able to overcome the
thoroughgoing historicism of the modern view of man as exemplified in the teachings of his own master, Heidegger. Given the significance that Heidegger carries in the pantheon of modern philosophy, and the degree to which his criticism of the doctrine of
anthropological constancy is taken for granted by the considerable
majority of modern or postmodern thinkers, this would be an error
of more than biographical importance. For what I have called the "integrity" of Jonas's thought, and, in particular, his refusal to evade the
difficulties inherent in the position that he came to maintain, would
be distorted and diminished if we did not seek to follow his own
path. Since the validity of his philosophy of nature, his anthropology, and his account of the objectivity of ethical judgment rests precisely on that integrity, and it is on these elements that my claims for
his broader significance rest, we must begin, as Jonas did himself,
with the challenge of understanding the enduring meaning of what
his first English book calls "The Gnostic Religion."

Actually, that title is itself somewhat misleading, for there is in
history no single, unified religion to which the name *Gnosticism*

might be applied. There was never a "pope of gnosis" dispensing a body of authoritative doctrine in which a body of believers were commanded, or otherwise enjoined, to believe. What there was was a variety of disputatious sects who shared, not a church or a doctrinal framework, but a body of beliefs that led them to regard earthly existence as intrinsically meaningless and to trust only in a special type of esoteric knowledge that led them to believe that, essentially, they were, by nature, in worldly, material terms—the standards of classical philosophy and modern science alike—other than they seemed to be.

The longer Jonas studied the phenomenon of Gnosticism, the more he was struck by the attitudinal parallels between its characteristic worldview and that of modern man as represented preeminently by the existentialism of Heidegger. Certainly there were considerable differences between the two, but, for all that, they shared certain common features rooted in a rejection of the idea, once embodied in classical Aristotelian philosophy and in the metaphysical worldview of traditional Christian orthodoxy, that the world could be understood as an innately meaningful totality in which man occupied a certain identifiable place from whose features he could deduce a proper normative pattern for his life. Much of Jonas's postwar work can be understood as an attempt to reverse this rejection in order to recover, for modern man, a means of ordering his life in conformity with what he can empirically know of his given place in the scheme of things. It is this project that achieves its completion in the ontologically based ethical system of *The Imperative of Responsibility* (1984), which represents the crowning achievement of his life and, in my view, his major claim to lasting fame as a philosophical guide to the dilemmas of our time.

Again, it is tempting to leap forward to examine the arguments of that remarkable work in which Jonas expounds his mature philosophy of responsibility in answer to the challenges of modern technology and its attendant dangers. But again the temptation must be resisted because the power of Jonas's argument is diminished if we fail to note the care that he takes to establish his case for the objectivity of ethical judgment in the face of the prevailing skepticism and moral nihilism of the age. And that case is rooted in his original attempt to understand the parallels between the existential nihilism of ancient Gnosticism and its modern equivalents in terms of a shared inade-

quacy of response to the binding features of the human condition and
their practical, ethical implications. Unless we follow the path of
Jonas's own response to that inadequacy, we will fail to see the extent
to which his philosophy represents not an arbitrary recapitulation of
an ancient metaphysics already undermined by the assaults of modern philosophy and the advances of natural science, but a renewed
recovery of a core of permanently valid existential wisdom that in-
corporates the very historical and scientific developments that have
rendered its original forms rationally unconvincing to the temper of
the times. There is nothing antiquarian in Jonas's synthesis, and if in
its defining contours we recognize a restatement of an essentially
Aristotelian philosophical realism, it is an Aristotelianism purged of
the burden of an outdated science and acutely responsive to just what
is most strikingly novel about our modern technological age.

We can, then, characterize Jonas's philosophy as at once emphatically modern and a philosophy of recovery and retrieval. It is modern both in taking full account of the findings of modern science, of
which he showed a grasp unusual among philosophers of his generation and background, and, at a deeper level, in facing head-on the
metaphysical implications of our present awareness that the universe, or cosmos, which once seemed so fixed and sure, is, in reality, a process of endless becoming, subject to physical entropy, and
in which nothing, however apparently secure, can be counted on to
endure unchanged. We may, with David Hume, speak of a constancy of human nature that underlies and conditions the changes that
have occurred in our history thus far, but, at a point in time in which
even that specific constancy has become subject to possible change
as a result of contemporary developments in biological engineering,
we cannot even assume the endurance of that relative constancy into
the future. What this means is that all that previous generations
could take for granted as providing a firm foundation, of which their
actions would have to take account, has become, in our day, only another field of flux, subject to alterations conditioned by our own
imaginations and all-too-potential actions.

It is just this development that best explains the urgency that
Jonas attaches to the element of retrieval in this thinking. What we
must retrieve is, first, a conception of practical philosophy, a sense
of what Aristotle called *praxis,* and which he associates, above all,
with the related spheres of ethics and politics, in which it is not only

the means but the end we have in view that is subject to decision. And second, again more deeply, we must cultivate in ourselves a sense of what the Greeks would have designated as cosmic piety, a presumptive respect for the innate structure, or ontological integrity, of things as they are in themselves. For it is on the persistence of such structures, not least of a habitable nature, or biosphere, that our own survival depends.

While our ancestors knew that though they would have continually to repair their city walls in order to sustain them against the ravages of time, they could take for granted the renewal of the natural world on which their life depended. We can no longer afford to make such an assumption, and nature has become for us a further province on whose sustaining order we can only rely if we learn to treat it with equivalent practical care. In recent years many writers have noted this development, but none, so far as I know, has seen so clearly as Jonas the extent to which the effectiveness of such care depends not on a romantic denial of the scope of reason but on its extension to the point at which it can encompass the end of cosmic preservation.

This is the new challenge of existence. On the one hand, it is unprecedentedly novel in its scope and, on the other, it requires of us a renewal of a precautionary wisdom of care that previously seemed apt only for those material and institutional artifacts— houses, cities, states—that man had constructed for himself. By and large, and in comparison with the ancients, modern philosophy has devoted relatively little attention to the logic of such care and the forms of reason appropriate to its effective exercise. As for science, it has taught us to manipulate ever more effectively, for good or ill, the things of nature, but on questions of purpose or goal it can say nothing. This is not to criticize the scientific enterprise nor demean the instrumental rationality that is at its core. It is only to say that, in comparison with science itself, philosophy, and practical philosophy or ethics in particular, has become a poor relation uncertain of the autonomous rational grounds on which it stands: unsure, indeed, as to whether any such grounds can be said to exist at all. It is the supreme virtue of Jonas's thought that he shows not only that there are such grounds but that they are, as Aristotle once supposed, both knowable and inherent in the very structure of nature that science has made its own.

Furthermore, Jonas is able to show that these grounds are open to a form of rational inquiry that is no less open to the objectivity of physical evidence than the experimental conduct of natural science. Such a conviction would not have seemed strange to the Greeks. But they supposed that the effectiveness of rational inquiry depended upon a cosmic structure composed of endlessly recurrent and constant elements to which the human mind was naturally ordered as one essential substance among subsisting others. This no longer corresponds to how we understand the universe; and to rest our claims upon a conviction that such an understanding is valid still is to fly in the face of all we have learned since the end of the Middle Ages. The challenge then is to reconstruct the integral rationality that characterized ancient and medieval metaphysics on the basis of an utterly different conception of what the cosmos can be said to be.

Among modern philosophers, Jonas has gone furthest in achieving this task; and he could do so, in part, because in his earliest work he encountered, and mastered, the original form in which the rational intelligibility of the cosmos was, so far as we know, first radically challenged. That form was the phenomenon of ancient Gnosticism, which, in the first centuries of the Christian era, set before man an image of the cosmos from which all trace of goodness, truth, and beauty, of mundane meaning and innate intelligibility, had been comprehensively removed.

It is this acosmism, amounting to a systematic denigration, rejection of, and spiritual rebellion against the innate order of things, including man's nature and place in that order, that Jonas sees as lying at the heart of the phenomenon of Gnosticism. And in this attitudinal stance, he perceives both its most striking original feature and its significance as a key to understanding later, contemporary modes of thought. In view of the importance Jonas attaches to the Gnostic reevaluation of the cosmos as inimical and, of itself, unintelligible to man except as something to be overcome, as well as to its exemplary import for the development of his own philosophical stance, it is worth dwelling a while upon what he has to say about it.

The term *cosmos* itself survives in current English usage as a near homonym for the Latin-derived word *universe;* when today we speak of someone as a "cosmologist," we normally mean a student of astronomy engaged, in the words of the *Shorter Oxford English Dictionary,* in understanding and explaining "the theory of the uni-

verse as an ordered whole, and of the general laws that govern it."
As for *cosmos* itself, it denotes something rather wider and less exclusively bound to the pursuit of a particular branch of natural science than the related *cosmologist*. A citation from 1650 explains that:
"As the greater World is called Cosmus [*sic*] from the beauty there-
of"; it is something of this original aesthetic sense, attaching to the
intelligibility of an encompassing, universal order, that is retained
in its evocative power in present speech. There is, at were, an aura
that attaches to *cosmos* that, while not necessarily mystical, seems to
suggest a sense of being that is more than everyday, material, or
mundane; and this sense is, perhaps, only confirmed when we look
at the literally extraordinary, extracommonsensical hypotheses and
notions—black holes, antimatter, and so on—that contemporary
scientific cosmologists invoke in seeking to make sense of their discipline. This in itself should serve as a useful reminder that rational
language can transgress the apparent bounds of normal experience
without becoming in any way divorced from scientific practice and
the use of human reason.

Thus, when we use the term today, we typically oppose *cosmos* to
chaos, by which we mean a state of meaningless or threatening disorder that could potentially disrupt and overwhelm the order of our
lives; when, in 1928, the philosopher Max Scheler sought to outline
a theory of man's being, or philosophical anthropology, that included, beside the facts available to history and natural science, an account of man's place in the totality of things, it is significant that he
entitled it "The Place of Man in the Cosmos," *Die Stellung des Men-
schen im Kosmos.*

In choosing this particular term, as opposed to *Welt* or "world,"
Scheler signaled his exemplary intention to provide, albeit speculatively, a theory that integrated the finite sphere of positive knowledge of the nature and condition of man—an anthropological "science" in the strict sense—with a wider perspective that opened into
questions of ultimate origins and destiny that are commonly reserved to religious discourse. The implication of Scheler's German
usage of *Kosmos* is exactly mirrored in its English equivalent to the
extent that when we hear someone use the term *cosmos* today, except
within the special sphere of academic astronomy, we are immediately inclined to suspect a more or less covert religious or otherwise extrascientific, metaphysical intention in what we are about to hear.

Once again consideration of terms is useful. Like *cosmos,* we derive our words *metaphysics* and *metaphysical* from the Greek, where originally they were applied to those books that succeeded, or went beyond *(meta-)* Aristotle's discussions of the physical world, his *Physics.* The *Metaphysics* were those writings that in their first, literal sense, came after the *Physics* in the corpus of Aristotle's philosophical system. By extension, *metaphysics* came to mean a theory of reality that extended beyond an account of the physical or material structure of the world with which natural science seeks to deal. In this sense, there is an intrinsic, evocatory relationship between the terms *cosmos* and *metaphysics* in common English usage; to the extent that anyone who is skeptical of the cognitive value of metaphysics, and who, like the logical positivists, regards it as a worthless undertaking unable to deliver anything beyond meaningless-because-unverifiable verbiage, is likely to become suspicious whenever the term *cosmos* appears in philosophical discourse in anything but a historical or astronomical sense.

Certainly, the idea that *cosmos* might denote, for us, as once it did for the Greeks, the awareness of an ordered, harmonious whole in which humans discover a meaningful place from which we can deduce an order of conduct appropriate to our condition is scarcely fashionable in current philosophical or, still less, political circles. Yet this is just what *cosmos* originally meant, and also what it can come to mean again if only we learn to use our reason in the face of current scientific knowledge with as much confidence and as fine discrimination as the ancients were prepared and able to do. But in order to accomplish this, we must understand and thereby overcome the legacy of what Jonas does not hesitate to call "existential nihilism," of which ancient Gnosticism and most modern philosophy are diverse, yet strangely affiliated, variants.

There is one further point to be made in explaining why consideration of the Greek semantic roots of the notion of cosmos, and of metaphysics as well, is important in the present context. This is Jonas's conviction that both the strange familiarity and the non-inevitability of an acosmism of a broadly gnostic type is best understood when it is set, not against the Christian-oriented metaphysics of creation deriving from a world-transcendent God, but against the worldview of Greek paganism. Many theologians, including Rudolf Bultmann, who had guided Jonas toward the study of Gnosis and whose own study *Primitive Christianity in Its Contemporary Setting* (1949) cites Jonas's prewar work, have argued that Christianity itself is in some ways a religion that draws on themes that, while not exactly gnostic, are very close to gnostic spirituality. This also is Jonas's view, and in *The Gnostic Religion* (278-81), he shows how even a Hellenizing Jewish thinker like Philo Judaeus, whose writings are contemporary with those of the earliest Christian as well as Gnostic texts, shows, in his discussion of the virtues, a distinctly quasi-Gnostic slant in the way he transforms the heritage of classical and stoic ethical thought. The point here is that although neither the church fathers nor Philo were Gnostics, their shared belief in a world-transcendent deity, before whose glory the worldly virtues of man were bound to seem inadequate, led them to adopt positions that would have seemed quite out of place in classical thinking and have an undoubted Gnostic resonance.

Here it will suffice to cite, with Jonas, Philo's view that "In ourselves are the treasures of evil, with God those of good alone" (*GR*, 280). Equivalent sayings can be found in the Christian canon and in the teachings of many of the church fathers. Since modern thinking can be argued convincingly, as it has been by such influential writers as Karl Löwith and Eric Voegelin, to be a consequence of an immanentizing secularization of an originally Christian worldview, it would hardly be surprising if, within modern thought, we found significant traces of apparently gnostic themes. Indeed, in Voegelin's writings of the immediate postwar years, notably his best-read work, *The New Science of Politics,* one even finds a characterization of revolutionary modernity, and utopian ideologies in particular, as an intrinsically gnostic phenomenon. This is not Jonas's view, and indeed the identity between activist political movements and the world withdrawal that is a feature of ancient Gnosis that Voegelin seems to suggest poses certain problems that his emphasis on a shared invocation of world-denying knowledge as a means of overcoming mundane order does not quite overcome.

That, though, is not the point I must stress, which is the extent to which Jonas's emphasis on the centrality of the existential acosmism of Gnosis, rather than on its claim to convey an otherwise unavailable yet essential knowledge of who, what, and why we humans essentially are, the doctrinal core of Gnostic teaching per se, leads him to contrast Gnostic thinking above all, not as Voegelin does,

with medieval Christian orthodoxy, but with the integral cosmic re-
ligiosity of ancient Greek paganism, to which it is, in a crucial sense,
much more radically opposed. The sense is crucial in the present
context because it explains why Jonas's studies of Gnosticism led
him, beyond themselves, in the particular direction they do: toward
a philosophy of nature, a philosophical biology, and a conception of
ethics that, while Kantian in form, is, in content, more akin to the
Aristotelian conception of ethics as a form of practical philosophy
bearing upon all those aspects of life over which we can and must,
at least potentially, exert our rational control.

Thus far, I have avoided the duty and pleasure of citing Jonas
directly, but now, as we seek to identify the cosmic vision against
which Gnosticism rebelled, we can do so no longer; for in his characterization of the mutually opposed Greek and Gnostic concepts of
cosmos we find an elegant statement of just what was at stake in the
Gnostic rejection of cosmic piety. "By a long tradition," Jonas writes,
"this term [cosmos] had to the Greek mind become invested with the
highest religious dignity. The very word by its literal meaning expresses a positive evaluation of the object—any object—to which it
is accorded as a descriptive term. For cosmos means 'order' in general, whether of the world or of a household, of a commonwealth or a
life: it is a term of praise and even admiration. Thus when applied to
the universe and becoming assigned to it as to its eminent instance,
the word does not merely signify the neutral fact of all-that-is, a
quantitative sum (as the term 'the All' does), but expresses a specific and to the Greek mind an ennobling quality of this whole: that it
is order. And indissoluble as this assignment of the term became in
time, and much as the emphatic form 'the cosmos' could denote only
the universe, it yet never came to monopolize the meaning and to
oust its other uses. Had these withered away, the name in isolation
from its original semantic range might have paled to the indifference
of the English 'world.' 'Cosmos' never suffered this fate. A manifold
of applications to objects and situations of daily life—applications
ranging from general to specific, from moral to aesthetic, from inner
to outer, from spiritual to material quality—remained in currency
side by side with the exalted use, and this co-presence of familiar
meanings, all of them laudatory, helped to keep alive the value-
consciousness which had first prompted the choice of so qualitative
a name for this widest and in a sense remotest of objects" (GR, 241–42).

Considered as cosmos, the universe was "the perfect exemplar of order, and at the same time the cause of all order in particulars, which only in degrees can approximate that of the whole" (*GR,* 242). In its sensible aspect, cosmos is beauty; in its inner principle it is reason; and, at the limit, with the Stoics, the cosmos is considered as in itself divine, the very form of God. And Jonas cites Cicero at length, in order to illustrate a particularly eloquent expression of this conception and one that explicitly draws out the way in which, so conceived, the cosmos comes to signify the source of man's ethical judgment as well as his biophysical form. "Man," Cicero writes, "was born *to contemplate the cosmos* and *to imitate* it; he is very far from perfect, but he is a little part of the perfect" (*GR,* 245).

According to this view, "The veneration of the cosmos is the veneration of the whole of which man is a part. The recognition of and compliance with his position as a part is one aspect of man's proper relation to the universe in the conduct of his life. It is based on the interpretation of his existence in terms of the larger whole, whose very perfection consists in the integration of all its parts. In this sense man's cosmic piety *submits* his being to the requirements of what is better than himself and the source of all that is good. But at the same time man is not just a part like other parts making up the universe, but through the possession of a mind a part that enjoys *identity* with the *ruling principle* of the whole" (*GR,* 246). Thus man seeks to adequate his existence to that of the whole and so learns from his rational appreciation of his situation to order his life in a way fitting to his nature and condition; and so, as a first-century A.D. author says: "Nature did not destine us for a base and ignoble existence but introduced us into life as if into a great festive gathering (like the Olympic games) that we might be spectators of their contending for the prices of victory and assiduous contenders with them ourselves." And if someone could look at the world from on high and behold the wealth of beauty within it, "he would soon know what we were born for" (*GR,* 247). It is this profound yet remote vision of the beauty and rationality of our possible worldly existence that characterizes the pagan worldview against which Gnosticism rebelled and of which the Christian, Thomist doctrine of the analogy between human and divine being, grand though it is, is but a metaphysically pale, attenuated reflection.

Compared with Gnosticism, the Christian ethics and metaphysics of creation, especially in its later quasi-Aristotelian form taught by St. Thomas Aquinas, preserves much of the pagan piety toward the integrity of mundane order and, with it, a sense that man can orient his worldly existence in accord with the right use of his God-given reason. Even so, it is, by virtue of its faith in a world-transcendent God and in the ultimate otherworldly destiny of the human soul, a fragile confection in comparison with the stoicism of a Cicero or a Seneca that is, by contrast, oriented toward the cultivation of world-ly virtue as the highest form of human fulfillment and perfection. In Thomism, the order of grace, now realized only after the passage from life to resurrection in heavenly bliss, perfects, without altering, the empirical and fatally flawed order of a nature in which man struggles through life against the burden of his fall from an original state of innocence in consequence of ancestral, original sin. By con-trast, Gnosticism represents a more radical break with the classical worldview, holding, as it does, that the created order—the world as we know it to be—is the creation, not of God, but of a flawed or ma-lign demiurge, or rebellious angel.

In such a creation, order itself is seen as a malign form of slavery from which no good can be expected or, except by means of spiri-tual escape, redeemed. It is beyond the scope of this book to recount the various speculative mythologies, some with quite horrendous narrative detail, by which the various Gnostic teachers explained the state of enslavement to the body and nature that they conceived mundane existence to be. Taken in sum, they represent a conceptu-al achievement whose pictorial equivalent is to be found, if at all, in the wilder fantasies of a Hieronymous Bosch in which all is pain and unreason incarnate—not so much a depiction of hell on earth as an identification of earth as essentially hell itself. The purpose of Gnos-tic myth is to explain how things came to be so, not as the result of human sin and imperfection, but of a cosmic catastrophe that pre-exists and predetermines the existence of finite human spirit, or soul, in the world, and to show how, by possession of esoteric knowledge, *gnosis,* the imprisoned spiritual substance of man can be liberated from bodily nature. In such a conception, there can be no such thing as a virtuous life ordered by right reason but only a des-perate effort to escape the bonds of finitude and enter union with purely spiritual being. Insofar as being is identified with the know-able qualities of existence, the state the Gnostic seeks is better de-

scribed as nonbeing; and Jonas, like Bultmann, notes the contribution that Gnostic doctrine made to the Christian discipline of negative theology, in which what is divine is identified only in terms of
what is not of this earth.

There is no question here of seeing modern nihilism as simply re-
producing the concrete form of Gnostic myth. Rather, Jonas claims,
it represents an equivalent existential stance rooted in a cognate experience of disorder and evil in the world and seeking to achieve
meaning through denial of the permanence, or ontological substan-
tiality, of that state of discomfort, anxiety and, at the limit, despair.
Equally, no possible answer to modern nihilism can take the form of
a literal restatement of the sort of cosmic faith that Plotinus could
avow in his reply to the Gnostic denigration of the cosmos. Modern
nihilism is emphatically modern, and any response to its challenge
must take on board the same range of knowledge and experience that
underlies the modern denial of the intelligibility and ethical validity of present order. Thus, while a neo-Platonist like Plotinus could
appeal to the eternal, unchanging form and beauty of the starry
heavens as warranting his belief in the essential goodness of the being that we know, his modern equivalent must seek his answers in
a world of cosmic and evolutionary process from which all perceiv-
able evidence of benign and immortal constancy has been definitively removed.

This is no easy matter, and therefore it is hardly surprising that
the modern temper should be characterized by an absence of ethical
and metaphysical certainty and a rejection of the idea that the objective world can provide, of itself, a measure of what we should
seek to make of our lives. If anything of the sort is to be done, it can
only be by way of showing, first, that nihilism is not the only logical, nor the best, response to the experience of universal flux and
second, that a world of processes that is itself in process toward an
indeterminate but nonetheless final end can supply us with firm
foundations for deciding the objective propriety of our acts. This,
and this alone, is the task and challenge faced by a philosopher who,
like Jonas, endeavors to outline an ethics for a technological age. In
attempting this task no step can be evaded and no evidence of its
potential impossibility denied. Rather, reconstruction and retrieval
must be attempted from the basis of the very existential reality that,
in the work of Heidegger and his successors, provides the warrant

for assuming that metaphysics is a spent discipline and, in its absence, we must either await the coming of an unknown god or, more commonly, simply make and mend as best we may with whatever technological tools we have at hand. Uniquely, so far as I know, Jonas, the student of Heidegger, and the once potential victim of the form of political nihilism that he chose lamentably to endorse, has faced this challenge and done so through the cultivation of the very forms of reasoning, practical philosophy, and metaphysics that his master considered defunct.

Like a host of fearful rabbits caught in the hungry eye of a fox, there is today a mass of self-styled theorists, in philosophy, the humanities, and even, one is led to believe by David Cooper, in nursing studies, who stand transfixed by Heidegger's figure, or at least by his renown, unable to say quite what he means yet unwilling to doubt that in his work he pronounced a death sentence on much of what previously had passed for sound philosophy and its once-intelligible discourse. In large part, the present vogue of uncritical postmodernity in which nothing is known for certain except news of the demise of metaphysics is a reaction from such sorry types to the impact of Heidegger's work on late-twentieth-century thought. It is not a reaction that Heidegger, who knew at least what metaphysics was and encouraged his students to engage passionately with the classic texts of its tradition, would have welcomed, but it is, for all that, an authentic response to a work that is, by turns, blindingly lucid and grotesquely and, as it seems, willfully obscure.

This is not the place to say what in Heidegger pertains to which category. The relevant literature is vast both in terms of Heidegger's own diverse writings and in the plethora of critically uneven commentaries they have provoked. Let it merely be noted that both George Steiner, in his 1978 Fontana Modern Master study, and, more recently, David E. Cooper, in his 1996 contribution to Claridge Press's Thinkers of Our Time series, have produced overall surveys of Heidegger's thought that manage to be at once brief, fair-minded, and lucid; and, except in the admirable concision of their critical accounts of a complex body of work, they are not alone. Let it also be said that among Heidegger's own students, there were several, Jonas not the least, who managed both to absorb his teaching and, as it were, to come out the other side in one intelligible piece as original, constructive, and relatively clear thinkers in their own right. Some of these I have mentioned before among Heidegger's notable Jewish students, but there were others, preeminently, perhaps, Hans-Georg Gadamer, the age's foremost exponent of the continuing viability of a hermeneutic reading of Platonic philosophy and thus, in one crucial respect, a necessary antithesis to the thoroughgoing anti-Platonism of Heidegger's own work.

In what remains of this chapter, I shall try to show how, starting from an existential orientation learned at Heidegger's hand, Jonas too began, through his comparative reading of Heideggerian existentialism alongside Gnostic acosmism, to develop just the sort of philosophy that Heidegger would, at first sight, have considered no longer tenable in his benighted age. There are two aspects of this undertaking to which I want to draw attention. The first is the general impact of Heidegger's existential orientation to philosophy on Jonas's early thought. The second is the way in which his Heideggerian formation conditioned his approach to Gnosticism and how, in turn, the study of the historical and attitudinal specificity of Gnosis allowed him to reflect back upon and, I shall argue, overcome the limits of Heidegger's existentialism. It is this last development that enabled Jonas to develop the distinctive ontologically informed practical philosophy of his latter years, one of whose features is, precisely, its retrieval of modes of thought that Heidegger, not to mention his uncritical admirers, believed he had consigned to history.

I shall deal with these in turn, beginning with the matter of what an existential orientation to philosophical interpretation meant to the young Jonas; in both, I shall be guided by a text, "Gnosticism, Existentialism, and Nihilism" (*GR*, 320–40), published as an appendix to his second (1962) edition of *The Gnostic Religion* but whose first version had appeared in the journal *Social Research* ten years before, and then, in expanded form, in German, in the theological journal *Kerygma und Dogma* in 1960. By Jonas's own high standards, "Gnosticism, Existentialism, and Nihilism" is not one of his most straightforward texts. It is, nonetheless, vital if we are to understand the original form of his thought, immersed as it was in the existentialism of Heidegger's *Being and Time,* and the way in which his parallel reflection on Gnostic and Heideggerian thought, the ancient and the modern, allowed him to outgrow this immersion and retrieve for his age what I have characterized as the implicit Aristotelianism of his late writings.

In my first chapter, I spoke of the "fatalism" of Heidegger's philosophy. By this I mean his tendency, especially in his later works, to present thinking itself as historically determined by what he calls the "History of Being." The effect of this is radically to historicize philosophy itself—to see in it not a free engagement of human thought directed toward the understanding and rational guidance of the human condition, but merely an expression of a historical movement directionally determined by fateful choices made in its past by the Greek founders of the metaphysical tradition of the West, whose final realization is the current age of global technology from which the effective autonomy of reason has been more or less definitively removed.

Heidegger's idea, expressed most powerfully in *The Question Concerning Technology* (1962), is that modern technology must be understood not as an autonomous practical effect of human ingenuity but as the ultimate consequence of developments inherent in the objectifying tendencies of Western thought. These are already implicitly present, pregnant with possibilities, among the ancient Greeks, and it is their consequences that work themselves out through history to culminate in the technologically conditioned circumstances of modern life. Put somewhat crudely, technology is thereby seen as the formative culmination of the objectifying reason of Western metaphysics—a potentially fatal climax, marked by what Heidegger calls a "forgetfulness of Being" from which, he claims, not practical reason but "Only a god can save us." This is a potent thesis whose tone is apocalyptic and whose effect is fatalistic in that it seems to remove from the sphere of current reason our every chance of regulating further the course of events. It is this that Jonas seeks to overcome in *The Imperative of Responsibility,* whose guiding theme is the retrieval of practical reason as a means of controlling the dynamic of technology and so preserve the integrity of man and the natural world on which his survival depends; it is just this possibility that Heidegger considers unattainable without some form of divine intervention for which we can do no more than prepare in a more or less grim mood of passive expectation.

Going somewhat beyond Jonas, we can see in Heidegger's historical fatalism a modern transmogrification of Gnostic cosmology in which the human situation is depicted as fatefully immersed in a drama of events over which we have, no longer, any effective rational control. With this distinction, that while ancient Gnosticism perceives this drama as determined supernaturally, by events that precede the appearance of man on the world scene, the result of the creative impulse of a malign demiurge, one who is innately opposed to a world-transcendent, spiritual, and alien God, Heidegger traces an equivalent effect to the unintended consequences of an originally human agency embodied, and first embedded, in the logic of objectifying metaphysical thought.

There is, in Heidegger, no equivalent to the Gnostic myth of an originally malign or flawed creation of cosmic order now seen in contrast to the Greek conception of cosmos, as less the support of man than the means of his enslavement to blind necessity. Instead, there is an account of the history of Being, no less enslaving, but now perceived as determined not mythologically by supernatural events but by the objectifying logic of an originally human choice of direction in the face of man's first encounter with the question of Being among the ancient Greeks. In both cases the result is a world order from which the efficacy of reason has been removed and in which man finds himself alienated and ineffective, no longer a lord of creation, nor even the governor of his own life, but the plaything of forces of which he has lost control.

Looked at in sum, what Jonas offers is nothing less than an alternative reading of this same history and situation, one that, in contrast to Heidegger's, preserves the integrity of philosophy as a means of comprehending and, potentially, regulating the course of events in accord with reason. It is a reading that begins from Heidegger's own telling account of the human condition but avoids the fatalism into which Heidegger fell after his abandonment of the existential ontology of *Being and Time* and the subsequent misguided adventure of his engagement with National Socialism in which, astonishingly enough, he perceived a movement capable of taking, once more, decisive control over the dehumanizing impact of modern technological civilization. While Heidegger responded to the miscarriage of his hopes with a retreat from reason and with a decision to place whatever trust remained in the fragmentary utterances of supposedly prophetic poets—Hölderlin above all, but also Stefan George, Georg Trakl, and others—Jonas responded to the same civilizational crisis, exemplified in the apocalyptic disaster of the Third Reich, not with a retreat from reason and science but with a renewed commitment to cultivate more broadly than before the heritage of rational thought.

In saying this, I do not wish to deny that the poetic turn in Heidegger's thought is, in its way, an undertaking rich in insights into aspects of Being untouched by the common run of reflective thought, a theme explored by Gerald Bruns in his book *Heidegger's Estrangements* (1981), in which he treats the relationship between language, truth, and poetry in Heidegger's late writings. Rather, I want to claim that to the extent that Heidegger disclaims philosophy for poetry as a vehicle for conveying the truth of Being, he abandons a field still rich with other insights that a more sober mind, like Jonas, can cultivate to considerable effect. It is as though Heidegger, moved by the weird logic of his own metaphysical radicalism, and by his impatient denial of the claims of science, betrays the promise that might once have made him the greatest metaphysician of his age—a man who might have fulfilled his first ambition to renew the question of Being in an antimetaphysical age and so guide his contemporaries through the dilemmas of their time. Fortunately, in Hans Jonas he found a student and a critic who was able to engage effectively and rationally the very questions that, in the later Heidegger, are abandoned to the automatism of a technologically oriented science to which he can only say "Alas," while waiting, like some latter-day John the Baptist, on a god who will not come. Put more soberly, if no less boldly, what I am suggesting is that it is in Jonas's project, not Heidegger's, that our best answers may be found.

Of Heidegger's impact on Jonas there can be no doubt. In "Gnosticism, Nihilism, and Existentialism," he writes of his initial assumption that the categories of existence that he had discovered in *Being and Time* had "a general validity, which would assure their utility for the interpretation of any human 'existence' whatsoever" (*GR*, 321). Guided by his friend and Heidegger's Marburg colleague, Rudolf Bultmann, he began his monumental study of Gnosticism. There, he writes, "I found that the viewpoints, the optics as it were, that I had found in the school of Heidegger enabled me to see aspects of gnostic thought that had been missed before. And I was increasingly struck by the familiarity of the seemingly utterly strange. In retrospect, I am inclined to believe that it was the thrill of this dimly felt affinity which had lured me into the gnostic labyrinth in the first place. Then, after long sojourn in those distant lands returning to my own, the contemporary philosophical scene, I found that what I had learned out there made me better understand the shore from which I had set out. The extended discourse with ancient nihilism proved—to me at least—a help in discerning and placing the meaning of modern nihilism: just as the latter had initially equipped me for spotting its obscure cousin in the past. What had happened was that Existentialism, which had provided the means of an historical analysis, became itself involved in the results of it. The fitness of its categories to the particular matter was something to ponder about" (*GR*, 320).

Out of this reflection emerged the insight that the applicability of Heideggerian existentialist categories to Gnosticism might not be the result of their general applicability to man's being as such, but of a historically specific parallel between the contingent circumstances, a homology of time and place, to which each seemed to answer. This led Jonas to the realization that "Existentialism, which claims to be the explication of the fundamentals of human existence as such, is the philosophy of a particular, historically fated situation of human existence: and an analogous (though in other respects very different) situation had given rise to an analogous response in the past. The object turned object lesson, demonstrating both contingency and necessity in the nihilistic experience. The issue posed by Existentialism does not thereby lose in seriousness; but a proper perspective is gained by realizing the situation which it reflects and to which the validity of some of its insights is confined" (*GR*, 321). Seen thus, the fundamental ontology of *Being and Time*, taken for granted hitherto, began to take on its true proportions as an account not of human being *(Dasein)* as such but of a particular contingent form of response.

This one might say was the antignostic *gnosis*, the saving knowledge, that delivered Jonas from his previous enmeshment in Heideggerian existentialism. The spell of what had seemed his cognitive fate was broken, as it were, in the realization that what had previously appeared to be an ontologically compelling account of human Being, an anthropology that veered between blind decision and resigned despair, might itself turn out to be no more than a particular, highly plausible, but ultimately unnecessary spiritual stance that was founded, not in the necessities of man's being as such, but in a combination of historically contingent circumstances that one particularly representative and articulate spokesman of his time had enunciated in the compelling prose of a great and powerful book. Heidegger was the spokesman and *Being and Time* the book that held a generation in awe, but they might, on further examination, prove to be only another chapter to be comprehended in a more rationally cogent account of the contours of existence. Whether such an account could, in fact, be achieved, and what form it might take, remained an open question, but what was indubitable was the realization that such a path was worth examining, especially because, to paraphrase some words from Ezra Pound, in Heidegger's world there was little or nothing "that made courage, nor made order nor made grace." Nothing guaranteed that an alternative account would be any more satisfying, but the chance was worth taking.

The uncanny parallels that Jonas had noted between ancient Gnosis and Heidegger's ontology, in both of which man was conceived as being flung (Heidegger's *Geworfenheit*) into the midst of a senseless, unstable cosmos, provided Jonas with at least the hope that such might not be the final word on the human situation. And if this was so, why should one take for granted Heidegger's other assurance that the days of rational metaphysics and objective ethics were finished in a world given over to the play of fate and power? Paradoxically, Heidegger had erected the antimetaphysics of *Dasein* analysis, in which man was said to have a temporal situation but no secure nature or being, *Sosein,* into an ersatz metaphysics of brute necessity without intrinsic meaning or rationality projected upon a cosmos of which he knew only that he was fated, uncomprehendingly, to die. That such a conception had deep historical and existential roots was clear enough, and Jonas made it his business to identify them and take them into account, but nothing that he found in his search led him to believe that they warranted acceptance of Heidegger's particular repertoire of responses, either that of his decisionism in the thirties or his subsequent fatalism. Rather, everything demanded another, more rational response.

Much of "Gnosticism, Nihilism, and Existentialism" is concerned with narrating the spiritual genealogy of Heidegger's existential nihilism in which Jonas perceives a development, beyond the point of breaking, of that tension between self and cosmos that already in the seventeenth century could lead even a Christian thinker like Pascal to write of his loneliness and fear in the face of the cold materiality of the new scientific cosmology. "Cast into the infinite immensity of spaces of which I am ignorant, and which know me not, I am frightened" (*GR*, 322). From this modern worldview, the sense of cosubstantiality between man and an earth-centered universe, in which God's noblest creation occupied a special place as first among his creatures, had vanished. "Gone is the *cosmos* with whose *logos* my own can feel kinship, gone the order of the whole in which man has his place. That place appears now as a sheer and brute accident." And so, continues Pascal, "I am frightened and amazed at finding myself here rather than there; for there is no reason whatever why here rather than there, why now rather than then" (*GR*, 323).

With the new cosmology and the displacement of man from its center, the human being loses not merely the ontological reassurance of knowing himself to be at home in a meaningful universe ordered in accord with his own God-given reason, but also the possibility of discovering an ethical measure in the intrinsic purposefulness of all that is. Nature now not only is immensely more vast in scale than anything he had previously imagined, but also is discovered to be devoid of innate purpose, a universe of pure and mindless extension as Descartes conceives it to be; this is fraught with consequence for a being who had formerly looked to its order as warranting the rightness of the choices he must make in the conduct of his life. "With the ejection of teleology from the system of natural causes, nature, itself purposeless, ceased to provide any sanction to possible human purposes. A universe without an intrinsic hierarchy, as the Copernican universe is, leaves values unsupported, and the self is thrown back entirely upon itself in its quest for meaning and value. Meaning is no longer found but is 'conferred.' Values are no longer beheld in the vision of objective reality, but are posited as feats of valuation. As functions of the will, ends are solely my own creation" (*GR*, 323).

It is this development—already prefigured in the evocative imagery of Matthew Arnold's magnificent but exemplary and desolate poem "Dover Beach"—that reaches its climax in the late nineteenth and twentieth century with the existential nihilism of Nietzsche and the decisionism of Heidegger, in whom the full sense of isolation in a heartless and soulless universe is registered in an existentialist philosophy from which all sense of objectively given value and meaning has been removed. This is the meaning and the measure of

modern nihilism with which contemporary man must cope as best
he may, and it is small wonder that, in such a world, the integral rationality of classical metaphysics should seem to have so little to say.
Small wonder, too, that every attempt to vindicate the objectivity
and universal validity of our sense of right and wrong should seem
so fragile a construction. For without the guarantee of an ordered
and purposeful cosmos, it is difficult to see how any claim to ethical
objectivity can be binding upon the boundless play of our desires
and all-too-native fears. Yet it is just this challenge that Jonas will
seek to meet in his projected ethics for a technological age, and here
he is encouraged by his observation that, though novel in form, contemporary nihilism and metaphysical skepticism is not without historical precedent. For at least once before, in ancient Gnosticism,
man conceived himself as flung helpless into a meaningless world
from which there could be no rational escape.

In his essay, Jonas points to the situational parallels, as well as the
differences, between the circumstances in which Gnosticism arose
and from which it drew its strength and those that condition the rise
of modern existentialism. What he says is brief but suggestive and
relates to the experience of a world of naked force in which the once
secure order of kinship, tribe, and polis had been shattered by the
rise and clash of great imperial powers during what Eric Voegelin
memorably calls "the ecumenic age." In comparison with Voegelin,
Jonas has relatively little to say about the political and social conditions in which not merely Gnosticism but other new forms of universalist religion, like Christianity, based around faith in a world-
transcendent God, arose against the background of the rise of no less
universalist empires. But he does point out that, in contrast to Christianity (or Judaism, Islam, and Zoroastrianism for that matter), Gnostic spirituality and faith in a transcendent deity is allied with a denial that this world forms any part of the pattern of divine creation
and that it is this, rather than its reference to divine transcendence
as such, that is the source of its distinctive, acosmic nihilism. This
is of central importance when we consider why, with the rise of
scholasticism, preeminently in its Thomist form, Christian orthodoxy was able to find a secure and central role for a rationally integrated notion of man's nature and place in the world, a metaphysics,
an anthropology, and a worldly ethics, that recalls the Aristotelian
conception of man's nature and place within his pagan cosmos. It is

only with the demise of this essentially Aristotelian cosmology that the challenge of nihilism is once more renewed.

I want to conclude this chapter by pointing out the significance of the fact that, despite the parallels between the phenomena of ancient Gnosticism and its modern, existentialist equivalent, we can take comfort in the observation that there is no continual historical chain that leads through time from one form of nihilism to the other. Rather, the path is punctuated by the long period in which Western thought was dominated by the rational metaphysics and cosmology of medieval scholasticism, which, preeminently in the philosophy of Aquinas, was able to reconcile a position of integral cognitive rationality with the new demands of belief in a world-transcendent God in whom alone the ultimate source of good could be said to be found. If Christianity could find a place for such a synthesis, is it impossible to imagine that the worldview of modern science could do the same and that, in Jonas, we may have a guide as to how this may be done?

Eric Voegelin once observed that what we require today is not yet one more Thomist revival but, rather, a new St. Thomas. Hans Jonas was a modest man and he would, I suspect, be somewhat shocked by my conjecture that there was about him and his achievement something of just this sort. By this I mean that just as Thomas renewed Aristotelian philosophy in a way that reconciled it with the theological orthodoxy of his age, so Jonas revives it while incorporating within its overall cognitive form the secured findings of modern natural science. Be that as it may, the mere fact of philosophical discontinuity—in which one age hostile to metaphysics can be succeeded by another more receptive to its ambitions, and so forth until the end of human time—testifies of itself to the possibility that the fatality of the history of Being, and, with it, of metaphysics, is by no means as unidirectional as a reading of Heidegger might lead us to suppose.

So long as human reason remains intact and the universe continues to offer the possibility of comprehension from within, so long does the possibility of metaphysics remain open. For, contrary to what is often asserted or assumed, the viability of metaphysics, and with it a rational ontology, an anthropology, and an objectively discoverable ethics based upon a grasp of what man must do in order to flourish, requires not complete knowledge of the ultimate beginning and end of the world process, but only the confidence to say what we know to be true about whatever is given for us to comprehend. The claim to totality of comprehension of all things visible and invisible, what may have been or is, perchance, to come, is a feature not of metaphysics in its authentic, Aristotelian, sense but of the fond or fearful imaginings of *gnosis,* the claim to know what is not known at all, that is the tempting but ultimately deceitful twin of philosophy and science alike.

Organic Being and the Philosophy of Life

We live in an age of academic specialization in which most of those who teach and do research in our universities are often rightly said to know more and more about less and less. There are many who defend this situation on the grounds that the growth of knowledge over the last century and a half has meant that the sort of encyclopedic knowledge that characterized the major thinkers of the past, and even the sort of range of general knowledge that an educated man in the nineteenth century might have been expected to possess, is no longer an available option, and that anyone who aspires to such an ambition today will inevitably be nothing more than a dilettante in each of the fields on which he presumes to speak or write. The hardening of disciplinary boundaries, the sclerosis of the arteries of debate, not only between the arts and the sciences, but within each of their component areas, combined with the massive growth in the number of specialized academic journals, each covering one small province of the sum of human knowledge, has meant that those who want to further their careers and ensure their professional reputations are almost forced to confine their attention to one small field of research if they wish to keep up with the current state of knowledge within their subject.

Add to this the fact that the growth of knowledge has been accompanied by a decline of general literacy and, with it, an increasing loss of a common tongue in which specialists in different fields are able to communicate their findings to each other and so engage in informed debate across their disciplinary frontiers, and you have a situation in which C. P. Snow's famous protest against what he called the division, and mutual incomprehension, between the "Two Cultures" of art and science seems, today, an unduly optimistic characterization. In academia today we have today not two cultures but an almost infinite multiplicity, each jealously guarding its frontiers against the incursions of outsiders, not least through the employment of its own arcane vocabulary, its house jargon, that renders its discourse all but incomprehensible even to those engaged in research in closely related areas. Reading now the biography of a Karl Marx, who read each year the Greek tragedies in their original tongue, or encountering the reflections of a Hegel or a Schelling on the implications of the science of their day, one is amazed at the range of their reading and the apparent depth of their expertise in areas that were not their own, as well as the degree to which they found it both desirable and necessary to inform themselves about such matters in order to be able to pursue their own particular vocations as philosophers.

And if this is true of philosophers, who traditionally have been regarded as specialists in the general body of human knowledge, on whom we depend in order to educate ourselves about the unified structure of our common world, how much more true is it of those whose academic work is, by choice or economic dictate, confined to the furtherance of research in one or other subset of the body of practical or theoretical knowledge? A figure who, like George Steiner or Roger Scruton, elects to compose and publish works across a wide range of disciplines, especially if he has the reputation of being a man or woman of strong or controversial opinions that he is not afraid to express, is treated with suspicion and not a little contempt by those whose ambitions are more narrow. Minnows are, not unnaturally, uncomfortable in the company of sharks, and in the same way those whose knowledge and interests are confined to their own minute fragment of the sum of knowledge are, by nature, suspicious of anyone who is not willing to be so constrained.

The institutional result of this state of affairs is encouraged by university structures where funding depends upon the repute in which their best-known faculty members are held by others educated in the same specialized field in consequence of the tyranny of the system of peer review. At best, this leads to a dissociation of educated debate across the common culture and, at worst, to an increasing plethora of departments dominated by charlatans whose reputation, and hence funding, depends upon an ability and willingness to communicate only with their fellow, more senior charlatans within a common field from which the potential judgment of outsiders is jealously excluded. In such an environment, self-interest and obscurantism flourishes, and the idea of a university that is, as John Henry Newman once conceived it to be, genuinely universal in its pursuit of common wisdom conducive to the good of humankind perishes in a world given over to the rule of those who no longer even presume to engage in what passes for intellectual debate. It is difficult to conceive when next we in the United Kingdom are likely to have a prime minister who could, like Arthur Balfour, presume to be a philosopher as well, and hard even to imagine a university that would be happy to employ a figure who, like Aristotle, presumed to know and teach both arts and sciences with equal application and might, for that very reason, put his colleagues to shame.

It will, of course, be said that given the range of our present state of knowledge such a presumption would be misplaced, the arrogant fruit of an immodest ambition to mastery of a range of knowledge impossible for anyone to attain today, but, plausible though such arguments may seem, nothing can justify the extent to which our universities are now, with rare exceptions, become multiversities, shelters for a host of ill-educated micropedists who pride themselves on their inability to communicate with their colleagues in other fields, still less the wider world.

In such an environment Hans Jonas was, even in his own day when the entropy of knowledge was not so far advanced as now it seems to be, a remarkable exception. He was by discipline a philosopher, schooled in the niceties of Husserlian and Heidegerrian research, and capable, when required, of holding his own in technical debate with his less cognitively ambitious fellows; his published work not only covered regions that ranged from the study of ancient myth to the prospective course of biological engineering but also, as I have already indicated, was composed in a literate and graceful prose innocent of that indulgence in jargon that is the bane of so much contemporary academic writing. Left to his own devices, without the impact that the rise of Hitler inflicted upon his career, Jonas might, I suppose, have remained a specialist in the history and philosophy of religion, read with care by his fellows in the field but known, if at all, to the world at large as one professor among others blessed with the good fortune to be paid a relatively healthy salary to pursue interests that, for others, might at most constitute a fascinating but economically unrewarding hobby, a pleasant distraction from the graft of financially necessary labor.

As it was, things did not turn out that way. Enforced exile and a chosen engagement in the bloody but too-often necessary business of war deflected him from the single-minded pursuit of an academic career and, at the same time, broadened his perspective on what the pursuit of philosophical inquiry required in the conditions of the modern world. At the same time, the habitual intellectual rigor that he had learned in an academic education in philosophy at the hands of Heidegger, perhaps the greatest teacher of philosophy if not always the wisest of philosopher of his age, and honed in his scholarly research in the unusually complex field of Gnostic studies, served him well when, through his response to the potentially fatal pressure of political events, he turned, in the face of immediately threatening death in battle, to the study of the phenomenon of life. There, as in his research into Gnosticism, he was not content to scrape the surface of received knowledge and take for granted the conclusions of others who had already plowed the fields of the relevant disciplines. Instead he set his mind to master the relevant science and, because he was first and foremost a philosopher sensitized by Heidegger to an appreciation of the anchorage of all authentic philosophy in the concerns of our mortal existence, to seek to draw from his knowledge conclusions relevant to the conduct of life. That he was able to do so in a manner intelligible to that increasingly rare creature, the generally educated reader is, I suppose, a function of an innate talent for clear speech. That he chose to do so testifies to his educated conviction, first, that both philosophy and science are matters of too much consequence to remain the property of academics alone, and, second, that the pursuit of one without the other is destined to result in a discourse and a practice potentially fatal to the future prospects of the race.

Both in his cultivation of stylistic clarity and in his insistence on the benefits of a mutual cross-fertilization between scientific research and philosophical reflection, Jonas thankfully departed from the example of Heidegger and, in doing so, created a body of work that is a standing reproach to all those epigones of the Freiburg master who inherit the rebarbative excesses of his literary style without anything of the reflective depth that may, perhaps, excuse the notorious obscurity of so much of what he wrote. Not everything that is philosophically deep need be stylistically obscure, as philosophers like Descartes, Hume, and more recently Santayana and, in a different way, Wittgenstein, are there to prove. And though it would be foolish and unduly demanding to require that every considerable thinker should also be an agreeable writer—where, after all, would philosophy be without the notoriously difficult prose of Immanuel Kant's *Critiques* of pure and practical reason?—it is surely not too much to require that a philosopher should at least attempt to advance his arguments with as much attention to style as to content.

It is this conviction that informs the manner in which Jonas wrote as surely as his matter is informed by the belief there is a place for philosophical reason in the age of science and a place for science in the reflective discourse of philosophy. Of all Jonas's writings it is in the essays collected in *The Phenomenon of Life: Toward a Philosophical Biology* (1966) that the harmonious unity between these two convictions is most amply displayed. While their subject matter is, in many ways, as deep and intrinsically complex as may be imagined—nothing less than an account of the specific difference of organic being, and, within that realm, of man, within a universe of energized matter—the mode in which they are written, though inevitably requiring close attention from the reader, evinces a literary gift that a novelist, and even a poet, might envy.

What, though, is a "philosophical biology"? And, given that biology is, like the other natural sciences, an empirical discipline apparently sufficient unto itself, what business does the philosopher have in presuming to encroach upon its territory? Can he, indeed, bring anything of worth to what is, after all, in comparison with his own unsteady and disputatious discipline, an astonishingly successful enterprise, replete with ever new discoveries, and able to command not only an awed respect, not untouched by fear, from the lay public but a degree of funding that would send even the most distinguished of philosophers scuttling to the bank to make sure that some distracted clerk or misprogrammed computer had not mistakenly added several zeros to the balance of his account?

To the first question Jonas gives a characteristically cogent answer that, in view of its heuristic value and the jealousy with which biologists, like other natural scientists, defend their discipline from the potentially disturbing interference of a presumptively uninformed lay public, is worth citing at length. As for the second and third, they can only be answered when we have examined the content of Jonas's book and, given the implications of biological science for the conduct of life, the field of ethics; perhaps not even then. Certainly they will be answered more fully only when we have included within our purview the ethical arguments of *The Imperative of Responsibility* to which we will come in good time, for it is in the nature of ethical judgment, at least as Jonas conceives it, that it proceeds not by arbitrary fiat or appeal to intuition but rationally and reflectively as befits an activity that bears upon our dealings with the facts of life.

Thus an ethics that presumes to pronounce on matters biological and the future conduct of the sciences of life—and Jonas does just this—cannot precede examination either of the nature of life itself, the distinctive structure of organic being, or of what is implied for the future of life, including human life, by current developments in biological science. The point is, or should be, obvious enough. Nevertheless it needs to be stressed because, though such issues are of evidently wide concern, as witnessed by debate over the genetic modification of foodstuffs, medical ethics, euthanasia, ecology, and a host of other areas, much of this debate is characterized by a degree of mutual incomprehension and blind suspicion between, on the one hand, researchers in the particular fields and, on the other, those members of the public troubled by recent developments, including the journalists and spokesmen for pressure groups who claim to speak on their behalf. The result too often is a dialogue of the deaf, which we can ill afford in matters so serious and fraught with consequence for us all.

It would be foolish to suppose that the considerations of any single philosopher, even one as well informed and discriminating as Jonas, could settle any of these issues. And anyway, it is in the nature of scientific research that it will always throw up novel problems, many of which, especially in the field of biology, will have considerable practical consequences for a living being such as man and therefore, quite properly, provoke concerned debate and dispute among those who believe they will enjoy or suffer the results. Then, too, Jonas alas is now dead, and it would be unreasonable to imagine that even a thinker as prophetically gifted as I take him to be could foresee even a small proportion of what these consequences may be. At the same time, if there is one thing that we can learn from his work it is that organic being as such, and the particular type of organism that is man, is structurally and existentially determined by certain features on whose maintenance and conservation its very survival depends. And these are relatively constant.

By "structural determination," I mean the combination of inherent features that make an organic being what it is. By "existential determination," I mean those aspects of the relationship between an organism and its sustaining environment, including, in the case of man, his social and political environment, that must continue to exist if its life is to continue. In the latter case—and now, with the development of possibilities in genetic manipulation, the former, too—consideration of such issues demands qualitative judgments that, by its nature, science alone is ill-equipped to make. Indeed, when the scientist pronounces on such matters, he does so with a rational equipment that is, in principle, no different from that available to any other rational and intelligent member of the human race. This is something that scientists are sometimes inclined to forget, but it is clear enough when we consider that what such judgments bear upon is not the conditions of organic survival per se but those under which an organism may flourish and so fulfill its innate potential. Here deliberation is of ends as well as means, and the rationality of such judgments does not depend on the untenable teleological assumptions of an Aristotelian science that assumed the innate purposefulness not only of each life form but of the cosmos as a whole. It is enough to know that an organism under certain circumstances will thrive and under others will wither and perish. Anyone who has ever tended a houseplant or kept an aquarium of tropical fish will know what I mean. In the case of human beings, who are supremely adaptable organisms able to survive in an extraordinary range of environments, the case is more complex than it is for the plant or fish, but the range of relevant considerations is in principle the same.

If a philosopher, trained, as one should be, to think clearly, is ill-equipped to pronounce on such issues, it is hard to say who is. But for this to happen, the philosopher must be prepared to conceive his vocation in a broader sense than is currently fashionable. That there are such philosophers, even in England today, is indubitable; interestingly and perhaps significantly, a strangely high proportion of those who have transgressed the boundaries of the prevailing conventions of the analytical school have been women. I think here of Mary Warnock, Mary Midgley, and the late Iris Murdoch in particular. But none of these, so far as I am aware, has approached the problem of a philosophical biology quite so broadly or so deeply as did Jonas—which brings us neatly back to our first question: What is a philosophical biology? Jonas gives the answer in the foreword to *The Phenomenon of Life*.

Jonas defines his theme as the attempt to offer "an 'existential' interpretation of biological facts." "Contemporary existentialism," he observes, "obsessed with man alone, is in the habit of claiming as his unique privilege and predicament much of what is rooted in organic existence as such: in so doing, it withholds from the organic world the insights to be learned from awareness of self. On its part, scientific biology, by its rules confined to the physical, outward facts, must ignore the dimension of inwardness that belongs to life: in so doing, it submerges the distinction of 'animate' and 'inanimate.' A new reading of the biological record may recover the inner dimension—that which we know best—for the understanding of things organic and so reclaim for the psycho-physical unity of life that place in the theoretical scheme which it had lost through the divorce of the material and mental since Descartes. Accordingly, the following investigations seek to break through the anthropocentric confines of idealist and existentialist philosophy as well as the materialist confines of natural science. In the mystery of the living body both poles are in fact integrated. The great contradictions which man discovers in himself—freedom and necessity, autonomy and dependence, self and world, relation and isolation, creativity and mortality—have their rudimentary traces in even the most primitive forms of life, each precariously balanced between being and not-being, and each already endowed with an internal horizon of 'transcendence.'" Jonas pursues this single theme as it develops through an ascending order of functions: "metabolism, moving and desiring, sensing and perceiving, imagination, art and mind—a progressive scale of freedom and peril, culminating in man who may understand his uniqueness anew when he no longer sees himself in metaphysical isolation" (*PL,* xi).

Aware of the suspicions such an undertaking may arouse, Jonas alerts his readers that in his work they will find nothing of the evolutionary optimism of the then-fashionable Teilhard de Chardin, nor of any other, better conceived, "metaphysical success stories" that picture life as a majestic march culminating in its sublime consummation in man. Instead, "He will find life viewed as an experiment with mounting stakes and risks which in the fateful freedom of man may end in disaster as well as success" (*PL,* x). Jonas's tools are, primarily, critical analysis and phenomenological description of the diverse forms of organic being, but, at the limit, he admits that he is prepared to engage in undemonstrable, but not therefore meaningless, metaphysical speculation on ultimate and humanly unavoidable questions of life's purpose. These, though, are not his starting point, which is reflection upon the facts of living being as disclosed by modern empirical science. For this no taste for speculation nor leap of faith is demanded or required.

Jonas is not unique among phenomenologically trained philosophers in turning his attention to questions of biology and their significance for our understanding of human nature. In 1928, Helmuth Plessner published a magisterial volume entitled *Die Stufen des Organischen und der Mensch (The Stages of Organic Life and Man)*, in which he endeavored systematically to understand the specificity of man's being against the background of an understanding of organic life; this is the central theme in his philosophical anthropology to which he returned repeatedly until his death in 1985. Plessner's book is one of the undoubted masterpieces of twentieth-century German philosophy, and it is a lamentable comment on the current state of what, in British and American universities, is called "continental philosophy" that while every last effusion of the Frankfurt School of neo-Marxism finds a ready market in English translation, Plessner's masterwork remains untranslated thus far, despite the fact that, like Jonas's reflections on man's place in nature, it represents a perspective on human affairs that is, in view of recent developments in science, if anything more vital to our self-understanding than when it first appeared.

Rather strangely, Jonas does not cite Plessner in his essays on philosophical biology and anthropology, though references are common enough to his teacher, Heidegger, whose defective, because biologically limited, ontology of *Dasein* Plessner criticized to great effect. Perhaps Jonas thought such references redundant, in which case I think that he was mistaken. At any rate, there is a certain, unsurprising family resemblance between Jonas's account of the biologically rooted uniqueness of man and that of the rather older Plessner that should not pass unnoticed.

Unlike Plessner's 1928 work, *The Phenomenon of Life* is not a single systematic treatise. Rather, it consists of a series of essays published from 1950 onwards, some of which appear also in Jonas's other books, and many of which are supplemented by appendices written later in which the author discusses issues related to the content of the preceding essay. Furthermore, some of these essays—for example, "Heidegger and Theology" and "Immortality and the Modern Temper"—extend the scope of the book far beyond the theme of a philosophical biology and the philosophy of life as such. Yet this should not lead one to suppose that the resulting volume is, like the 1974 collection, *Philosophical Essays,* an anthology of related writings covering the full range of the author's interests. True to Jonas's conception of what a philosophy of life entails, the essays are grouped successively in a logical sequence that follows the logic of emergent life from its origins in the simplest most primitive forms of organic being to its culmination in the unprecedentedly complex form of human existence.

It is this logic that gives unity to the whole and makes of the work a more than adequate substitute for the systematic statement that, in 1966, Jonas still apparently intended to write but never did. Indeed, since his study of the increasingly complex forms of life eventually opens out onto the problem of ethics—the theme of *The Imperative of Responsibility*—little or nothing is lost of the unity of the project. One may even say that, in view of his mastery of the essay form, the fact that Jonas's philosophical biology is laid out in a succession of discrete chapters, each complete in itself, is an advantage to the reader, permitting him to grasp more surely the stepwise approach by which his argument proceeds. What might otherwise have been a forbiddingly extended argument directed against the apparently unbridgeable dualism between matter and mind, the realm of spirit and the physical form of the world, that has dominated Western philosophy since Descartes becomes, in *The Phenomenon of Life,* a more manageable adventure in which we are lead by relatively easy stages through the reflective steps by which that dualism can be overcome. Furthermore, the fact that the book is composed of essays allows Jonas to discuss themes such as the inadequacy of understanding purpose in terms of cybernetics, or Sir James Jeans's hypothesis that the ultimate structure of the world can be understood in terms of mathematics—the naturalistic and materialist assumption inherent in the claim that ontology, the theory of being, can be reduced to questions of physics—that would, in a systematic treatise, distract us from the overall thrust of the argument.

As it is, Jonas's reliance on the essay form permits us to take one step at a time and emerge from the experience with the conviction that the antinaturalist position that he maintains requires no sacrifice of rationality and no flight from empirical knowledge into the cloudy heights of romantic assertion or the subjectivity of an appeal to intuition. In this, Jonas's philosophy of nature is immeasurably superior to its nineteenth-century predecessors, like Schelling's, and even to such twentieth-century models as Whitehead's philosophy of the organism, in which one has the impression that the field of science is philosophically comprehended by one or another intellectual sleight of hand. Such constructions may give comfort to those already convinced that natural science cannot, of itself, be taken to provide us with a total account of reality, but, in an age in which science enjoys a quite justified preeminence within the field of knowledge based upon its practical achievements as realized in current technologies, they can scarcely be expected to carry conviction either with scientists themselves or with those who look predominantly and, at times, exclusively to science to provide them with solutions to the practical problems of their lives.

Today we can only smile at the sublime but arrogant confidence that could lead Hegel to remark, when faced with the discrepancy between the implications of his dialectical reason and the evidence of the facts, "So much the worse for the facts." Such a form of integral rationalism, supremely self-assured of its own cognitive worth as a level of science founded in reason and qualitatively superior to mere empirical inquiry, must, in a world from which residual belief in providential progress has all but vanished, now seem little better than a superstitious leftover, a secularized echo, from an age of faith of which, in the words of Arnold's "Dover Beach," we now hear only "its melancholy, long, withdrawing roar." If then we are not, like Arnold's lovers, to be left—true, perhaps, to one another, but otherwise alone—"on a darkling plain . . . Where ignorant armies clash by night," we require another form of response than that of a fideistic progressivism no more currently credible than the teleological cosmology of Aristotelian natural science, in which everything was assumed to be directionally inclined toward its proper and humanly intelligible place, or the hardly less intelligible neo-Platonic belief in the Great Chain of Being. Of its nature, such a response can evade neither the implications of modern science, nor the universal contingency that this science implies, but must instead incorporate just these implications. And here the Aristotelian project is indeed exemplary, based as it was on a sure grasp of and respect for the best science of his time. It is this example that Jonas follows in *The Phenomenon of Life*.

By way of preface to the essays, Jonas begins with a brief introduction, "On the Subjects of a Philosophy of Life." Such a philosophy "comprises the philosophy of the organism and the philosophy of mind. This is itself the first proposition of the philosophy of life, in fact its hypothesis, which it must make good in the course of its execution. For the statement of scope expresses no less than that the organic even in its lowest forms prefigures mind, and that mind even in its highest reaches remains part of the organic. The latter half of the contention, but not the former, is in tune with modern belief; the former, but not the latter, was in tune with ancient belief: 'that *both* are valid and inseparable is the hypothesis of a philosophy which tries for a stand beyond the quarrel of the ancients and the moderns'" (*PL*, 1). No statement better conveys what I meant when I claimed, in my first chapter, that Jonas's is at once an emphatically modern philosophy and a philosophy of retrieval.

Without recognizing the rootedness of mind in the organic processes of the brain, and of the composition of brain from chemical elements compounded in that peculiar way that allows for the self-renewing processes of organic being, living tissue, we would fail to take on board the lessons of modern science. But equally, if we cannot see that the apparent autonomy of mind is in some identifiable way prefigured, or prepared for, in properties pertaining to organic being as such, we will fail to understand the distinct specificity of animate as opposed to inanimate matter. It is just this that the dualism of Descartes, according to whom matter has no other property than physical extension and mind no physical property at all, fails to recognize. And though modern biological science is not exactly Cartesian, or does not at least recognize itself as such, the concept of matter with which it operates, derived from chemistry and thence physics, is one that identifies matter, the stuff of compounds, with what can be measured alone. Thus, though biology can describe the processes of life, it cannot readily identify in what life consists.

This is not a genetic question of when or how life originates, but a morphological one concerned only with what it is. The question of life's origin may be answered or may remain mysterious. Either way one says nothing essential about that in which its specificity consists. Equally, an adequate description of the properties of living being is independent of an adequate understanding of how it develops through time. Mankind did not need the evolutionary theory of a Darwin in order to understand the qualitative difference between living and dead matter. Evolution is not classification, and sound classification requires no knowledge of evolution. This, again, is an obvious point but no less important for that. Recognition of its significance helps us to understand what one may call the implicit metaphysics of our apparently antimetaphysical age as well as the way in which Jonas's philosophical reflections help us to overcome the inadequacy of the covert assumptions embedded in a metaphysics that no longer recognizes itself as such.

In 1981 the MIT Press published a translation of a collection of Hans-Georg Gadamer's essays under a title—*Reason in the Age of Science*—that could, equally, serve as an overall motto for Jonas's work. Gadamer is, as Jonas was, a philosopher "formed," as Jonas says, "during the 1920s in the school of such teachers as Husserl, Heidegger and Bultmann." He is best known for his treatise *Truth and Method,* which is rightly regarded as the foremost statement of what is called "hermeneutic philosophy." The term *hermeneutics,* derived like *philosophy* from the Greek, has received wide currency in recent years among practitioners of what is commonly called "continental," as opposed to supposedly Anglo-Saxon "analytical philosophy," itself the gift to the British philosophical establishment of such well-known "Anglo-Saxons" as Wittgenstein and the exiled theorists of the Vienna Circle! As such, it has come to be regarded as a somewhat mystifying term emblematic of a style of thinking undisciplined by the requirement for conceptual clarity and modesty of purpose in which British philosophers in particular take such pride.

The fact that hermeneutic philosophers, in contrast to their analytical colleagues, commonly hold the notoriously obscure Heidegger, rather than Wittgenstein, to be the foremost thinker of the twentieth century, combined with the historical truth that it was indeed Heidegger who, in *Being and Time,* defined philosophy in essentially "hermeneutic" terms as concerned with establishing the "fundamental ontology of *Dasein,*" man's situation of being-there-in-the-world, and that his own elaboration of this theme is so reputedly elusive, has resulted in a widespread failure to perceive that the central claim of hermeneutic philosophy is, in fact, both simple and convincing. It is that philosophy is, in sum, nothing other than the business of reflecting rationally upon and interpreting the empirically given reality of the human condition. The fact that Heidegger himself made such heavy weather of this enterprise, and that many of his avowed followers have seized on just what is most mystifying in his work, should not allow us to forget the inescapable simplicity of the truth that lies at its core: Human beings—the selves we know ourselves to be—find themselves on an earth in which they must orient themselves reflectively in order to survive. Sound practice is the fruit of such reflection.

Put simply, hermeneutics is the practice of reflective interpretation, and a hermeneutic ontology of human being is a philosophy that concerns itself with understanding man's nature and place in the world. Any philosophy that forgoes such an ambition betrays its own native vocation and, in doing so, fails to be what alone can justify its existence as the pursuit of rational inquiry. What, if anything, then distinguishes philosophy from science, which also aspires rationally to describe and explain reality? The only coherent answer to this question that I can see runs as follows. Science is, as it were, a primary, first-order activity whose object is investigation of the phenomena of the world. The natural sciences, physics, chemistry, and biology, study the factual properties of the phenomenal world as man finds it to be. The cultural and social sciences, what the Germans call the *Geisteswissenschaften,* in which we include history, sociology, and much (though not all) of psychology, rooted as it is in the study of that portion of the organism we call the brain, take as their province what man makes, has made, and may potentially make, of that world and the chances it affords. As for philosophy, it is a second-order reflection upon what the sum of knowledge, in which we include not only the findings of science in all its manifold disciplinary varieties but also the evidence of our commonsense perception of reality, may convey.

Philosophy is therefore an integrating discipline whose purpose is the generation of an understanding of the totality of the world that man inhabits and in which he must make his way. Metaphysics, or, as it has been called since the seventeenth century, ontology, is the theoretical account of that integrated understanding of reality. Ethics is the no less rational attempt to determine the desirability or otherwise of ways of dealing with that reality in accord with what we know to be the conditions in which human beings can flourish. As ontology reflects upon the data of common sense and science, seeking, through critical evaluation of their significance, to offer an overall understanding of the real, so ethics reflects upon the datum of ontology with a view to guiding the future course of human practice. Ontology is an interpretative, or hermeneutic, account of the facts of life—what Heidegger, in one of his lecture courses, called (with characteristic lack of stylistic grace) a "hermeneutics of facticity." Ethics is a practically oriented interpretation, a hermeneutics of what, actually or potentially, the facts of life allow to one who dwells within their framework. Ontology and ethics are together two successive levels of reflection in which philosophy consists. And as ethics is blind, empty of cognitive content, without ontology, so ontology is uninformed without awareness of what science and commonsense perception convey.

Jonas is a philosopher in just this integral sense. He offers an ontology and an ethics founded in reflection upon the sum of what we presently know to be man's current and prospective state. Unlike Heidegger, the informational content on which he reflects includes the data of contemporary science, which, for reasons we cannot examine here, Heidegger dismisses as derivative and of secondary importance. This makes Jonas's "hermeneutics of facticity," a phrase that on grounds of its stylistic infelicity alone he would reject, both more inherently rational than Heidegger's and more plausible and acceptable to an audience impressed, even when it does not understand, by the modern, scientifically informed worldview. Whether it is any more true I leave to my readers to decide. At any rate, given the significance of current developments in biological science, and the awed and fearful attention with which they are regarded in popular perception, it is difficult to imagine any body of philosophical writing that is more relevant to public concerns than the collected essays of *The Phenomenon of Life.*

Nor is their relevance confined to the extrascientific lay public. For scientists, too, have much to learn from Jonas's reflections, informed as they are by a level of philosophical sophistication, an appreciation of those questions that science alone cannot answer, that is untaught in the formation of those in whom the conduct of scientific research is vested. To be a professional scientist requires both considerable intelligence and a long apprenticeship in intrinsically difficult areas of study, less perhaps in biology than in theoretical physics but of each a great deal nonetheless. But nothing in the educational formation of even the most intelligent professional scientist equips him to be anything more than an amateur philosopher. Indeed, there are two unrelated factors that frequently contribute to making the scientist an even less competent philosopher than an intelligent lay observer of the scene. The first is the degree to which a scientific education requires a level of sustained intellectual commitment, an exclusivity of attention, that precludes a cultivation of other, no less mentally demanding, engagements. The scientist may relax by fishing or listening to music. He may even become a skilled fisherman or a passably competent musician—many in my experience are—but what he is unlikely to do is to divert himself from the study of scientific papers and the devising of research programs by boning up on the equivalent complexities of philosophical discourse. The second philosophically disabling factor in scientific formation is the extent to which the cognitive framework of modern science itself embodies unspoken and ill-considered philosophical presuppositions of its own.

Nowhere is this more true than in the field of biology, where it is commonly assumed that the theoretical framework of Darwinian evolution provides of itself an adequate philosophy of organic being and that this, in turn, implies acceptance of a materialist metaphysic. It is not rare to find theoretical physicists who are at least open to the plausibility of metaphysical and religious beliefs whose assumptions transcend the limits of force-governed philosophical materialism. Indeed, the nature of modern physics, of cosmology above all, seems to require a willingness to entertain hypotheses and notions inexpressible in conventional materialist terms; this may explain why there are, in our universities, rather more physicist-theologians than their biological equivalents. Be that as it may, contemporary biology is, even in comparison with other scientific fields, an arena in which there reigns a form of materialism with which neither Helvétius nor the late Friederich Engels of *The Dialectics of Nature* could have found much fault.

In biology, as elsewhere, fashionable ideas come and go. Sociobiology, the mantra of the seventies, has been displaced in the current imagination by fables of the selfish gene and the conjectures of what now is called "evolutionary ethics." What remains constant is the assumption not only of the philosophical adequacy of Darwinism in accounting for the nature of life but, more seriously and less convincingly, the materialist metaphysical implications that the evolutionary hypothesis is taken to presuppose. No one in Britain at least can switch on the radio and hear, as frequently he will, the voice of so distinguished and urbane a biologist as Lewis Wolpert without being reminded that in organic science the idea that another view is worth hearing is loftily dismissed as unworthy of serious consideration. And, if this is true of a culturally informed figure such as Wolpert, how much more true must it be of the host of lesser men and women to whom, through medical and more general biological research, our fate is consigned?

What is in question here is not the validity of Darwinism as such, which, Jonas insists, remains the most convincing account we have of the mechanism by which life forms emerge and pass out of existence. No one need fear that Jonas requires of his readers any conversion to the sort of "scientific Creationism" that, though popular in the United States, finds few exponents this side of the great Atlantic sea. And this is just as well because, for all the ingenuity with which it is dressed in scientific garb, so-called Creation science is, in reality, neither consonant with the present state of scientific knowledge nor required by a theologically orthodox reading of Judeo-Christian scripture, and only a linguistically underinformed literalist could suppose it so.

In theology, as in much of science, not least the further reaches of contemporary cosmology, such literalism is almost invariably out of place for reasons any medieval student of St. Thomas's doctrine of the analogy of being would have understood. It rests on an inability or unwillingness to take account of the inevitably symbolic and metaphorical functions of language as such, including, in the case of the biblical story of Creation, the language in which, it is believed, the story of divine cosmogenesis is conveyed to the human believer in terms that he can understand. Inevitably such a supernatural, transexperiential event as God's creation of the universe and all that is therein from nothing requires what we may term an analogical translation of its events into a natural language whose literal sense is derived not from Creation itself but from the forms of the already created order that we experience. But that is another story on which we shall dwell no longer. Jonas's object of criticism is, after all, not the misplaced concreteness of Creation science but the no less mistaken and more influential metaphysical materialism assumed in most contemporary interpretations of Darwinian evolutionary thought.

In the remainder of this chapter, I shall endeavor to summarize the reasons that Jonas gives for the origin and persistence of these assumptions, and why they are mistaken and can be shown to be so in the light of insights into the evolutionary continuity of life forms that are, somewhat paradoxically, native to Darwinism itself. I shall conclude by sketching the philosophy of the organism that he advances in opposition to the prevailing materialism of biological thought. For the first, the crucial text is Jonas's essay "Philosophical Aspects of Darwinism," which forms the second chapter of *The Phenomenon of Life*. For the second, I shall rely largely, but not exclusively, on observations that he makes in his third chapter, "Is God a Mathematician?" Taken together, these considerations vindicate his argument for the essential specificity of organic being as something irreducible to the physicalist assumptions of a materialist metaphysics that interprets all being in terms derived from the properties of inorganic matter. This is the aspect of his philosophy of life that is, as Jonas says in the introduction to his book, in tune with ancient but not modern belief, and therefore the crucial point that he must establish if he is to fulfill his ambition of achieving a philosophy that stands "beyond the quarrel of the ancients and moderns" (*PL*, 1). It is on his success in achieving just such a philosophy of the specificity of organic being as such that his further ideas in philosophical anthropology, and then an ethics that encompasses responsibility for nature as a new, extended categorical imperative, must depend.

In his essay on Darwinism, Jonas begins not with discussion of evolutionary theory itself but with an account of the new model of nature that in the seventeenth century displaced the older cosmology of Aristotelian physics and natural philosophy. Whereas the previous view had understood the universe, animate and inanimate bodies alike, as a complex of substances each identifiable as a specific, qualitatively unique compound of form and matter providentially determined to occupy a particular place in the cosmic order and centered hierarchically around the earth, and around man as the essentially highest form of earthly life, the new conception, inspired by the Copernican revolution in astronomy but whose philosopher was Descartes, was resolutely mechanistic. In place of the ancient idea that each being represented a particular individuation of its God-given essence came the new idea that "Each structure as found was conceived as a functioning mechanism whose analysis into elementary components of matter and motion was to explain its actual functioning by a uniform standard" (*PL,* 38). That standard was measurement.

Descartes was the central philosopher of this view, and to his essay Jonas appends an analysis of "The Meaning of Cartesianism for the Theory of Life" (*PL,* 58–63). Descartes was crucial to the new view of nature because by his dualistic division of the world into extended matter and immaterial spirit, the property on earth of man alone, he provided a simple, powerful metaphysical conception that reduced the manifold qualities of existing beings to two alone. In this way, extrahuman nature came to be seen solely in terms of its measurable properties. This gave a powerful impetus to the development of the mathematizing sciences of nature, but it was, from the start, beset by certain problems that were not easily solved, not least in explaining how it was that immaterial spirit could act upon the alien world of matter—what Arthur Koestler described as the mystery of "the ghost in the machine." Neither Descartes nor his successors could give a satisfactory solution to this problem, but such was the fertility of the conception in furthering scientific advance that its intrinsic philosophical difficulties were overlooked or answered in one or another ad hoc fashion satisfying only to the theorist who had devised it. Of these the occasionalism of Malebranche was at once the most intellectually consistent and the most intelligibly far-fetched in seeing, in each instance of nonmechanical movement, an occasion of divine, purposeful intervention in the universal mechanism in which the universe was now thought to consist. Rational and consistent though it was, occasionalism was an ontology that made the occurrence of miracles the rule rather than the exception to the order of being.

In one sense, Cartesian philosophy was a philosophy of process, recognizing in each being a system of thrust and counterthrust rather than, as Aristotle had believed, an instantiation of an endur-

ing essence. But while this mechanistic ontology explained the actual operation of existing structures, of itself it said nothing of how
any such structure came to be what it was. In this way it avoided potential conflict with the theology of divine Creation. And insofar as
it implied that the world as a whole could be envisaged as a total
mechanism made up of mechanically structured moving parts, it
allowed for, and indeed required, the postulation of an original,
world-transcendent designer—a divine "clockmaker"—who had
set it up in the first place and given it its ordered motion. This was
the worldview of eighteenth-century deism that still, in the next
century, inspired the natural theology of Paley that the young Darwin so esteemed. In this manner a mechanist ontology of matter
could explain both the functional operation of each of its moving
parts, organic and inorganic, and the overall movement of the whole
by invoking a literally supernatural originating principle readily
identifiable with the Christian creator God.

The revolutionary impact of Darwin's own hypothesis lay in the
fact that, by invoking the mechanism of natural selection, it provided a naturalistic explanation of how the forms of organic life,
plant and animal, could manifest the appearance of design and purpose. While previously the apparent harmony between the needs of
an organism and its provisioning environment could only be explained in terms of their purposeful design, now they could be understood as the result of chance mutations from which only the
fittest would survive. What had before seemed the fulfillment of divine purpose could now be explained in terms of chance variations,
most of them damaging to the individual's prospects for survival
but which could on occasion result in the emergence of life forms
more suited to endure and reproduce. In this way, Darwinism extended to organic nature—always a problem for Cartesian mechanistic philosophy—the blind play of purposeless force that already
served to explain the workings of the inorganic world. At the same
time, as Jonas notes, because the origin of man himself needed no
longer to be seen as an exception to this general rule of intrinsically purposeless process, there emerged the possibility of overcoming
the absolute distinction that Descartes had established between human mind and material nature: "The *continuity* of descent now established between man and the animal world made it impossible any
longer to regard his mind, and mental phenomena as such, as the

abrupt ingression of an ontologically foreign principle at just this point of the total flow" (*PL*, 57).

This, in foreshortened and thus inevitably oversimplified terms, is Jonas's account of the philosophical significance of Darwinism and of the place that the mechanistic ontology of Cartesian physics continues to play in its worldview. It is just this latter aspect of the matter that current biological science continues philosophically to emphasize to the exclusion of its other aspect—the reestablishment of the continuity of all forms of organic being. But this is only half the picture that emerges. For, as my last quotation from Jonas indicates, Darwinism is a philosophically ambivalent theory. On the one hand, it provides a way of conceptualizing the evolutionary phenomenon of life without recourse to the activity of intention or design, and in this way it succeeds in extending the logic of pure mechanism into the sphere of organic being as no previous form of Cartesian ontology had been able to do, faced, as it was, with the apparent evidential ubiquity of purpose in the functionally efficient forms of plant and animal life. But, on the other hand, it reestablishes the continuity of all forms of organic being through its theory of evolutionary descent and so, almost despite itself, overcomes the rupture between mind and matter—the metaphysical isolation of man—that characterizes Cartesian dualism.

"Thus," Jonas observes, "evolutionism undid Descartes' work more effectively than any metaphysical critique had managed to do. In the hue and cry over the indignity done to man's metaphysical status in the doctrine of animal descent, it was overlooked that by the same token some dignity had been restored to the realm of life as a whole. If man was the relative of animals, then animals were the relatives of man and in degrees bearers of that inwardness of which man, the most advanced of their kin, is conscious in himself. . . . [A]fter the contraction brought about by Christian transcendentalism and Cartesian dualism, the province of 'soul,' with feeling, striving, suffering, enjoyment, extended again, by the principle of continuous gradation, from man over the kingdom of life. What both Spinoza and Leibniz had enunciated as an ontological postulate, the principle of qualitative continuity, allowing for infinite gradations in obscurity and clarity of 'perception,' has through evolutionism become a logical complement to the scientific genealogy of life. The highest could have been reached from the lowest only through all intermediary stages, whether these were merely transitional or left in being as permanent representatives" (*PL*, 57–58).

It is this fact that vindicates, against the metaphysical isolationism of Cartesian dualism and the no less isolationist ontology of Heidegger's existential analysis of *Dasein*, the plausibility, indeed the necessity, of situating reflection on man within a comprehensive philosophy of life.

In a footnote pregnant with implied significance, Jonas observes that, in Darwinism: "Even the Aristotelian biological hierarchy of 'souls' is in a way restored under the form of genealogical sequence: the evolutionary 'later' largely coincides with the Aristotelian 'higher'" (*PL*, 58). Thus while a Heideggerian reflection upon man's being, a fundamental ontology of *Dasein*, can proceed in isolation from an account of organic being in consequence of its insistence on the uniqueness of man's mode of being in the world, it can do so only by denying the relevance of what we know of the essential features of other forms of organism. In view of what we do know of the innate and universal features of organic being by virtue of scientific inquiry, this is philosophical obscurantism of a high order. Plessner makes somewhat the same point when he observes that Heidegger's characterization of *Dasein*, in terms that privilege man's constitutive awareness of his own mortality—his being-unto-death—makes little sense if we do not also observe that only a living being, a form of organism, albeit one unique in his possession of a reflective awareness of his existential state, is even capable of such an awareness, and that, as he puts it in *The Stages of Organic Life and Man*: "An idea of the mode of existence of the human being as a natural occurrence and as a product of the history of his mode of existence can only be obtained by contrasting it with the other forms of animate nature that are known to us" (xix).

Equally, as Plessner's reference to the heuristic significance of "contrast" illustrates, what reference to the general properties of animate nature permits is not dissolution of the unique features of human being—the specific qualitative difference of human as opposed to other forms of animal being—in a general philosophy of the organism, but clarification of the precise qualities of these features as we know them to be. In "Change and Permanence: On the Possibility of Understanding History," an essay that, notably, appeared first in the *Festschrift* published on the occasion of Heidegger's eightieth birthday, Jonas endeavors to do just this in terms of the three expressive dimensions of tool, image, and tomb that characterize the human, as opposed to other forms of animal, being. These dimensions, present wherever we find evidence of identifiably human life, serve to warrant our assurance that though human beings are animal organisms, biologically related to and, in the case of the chimpanzee, almost genetically identical with other cognate, preceding, and existing forms, they are organisms of a quite distinctive kind. A mathematizing natural science of life will note that 98 percent of human genes are identical with those of the chimpanzee, but it fails to see the qualitative difference that the remaining 2 percent must make.

A philosophical biology, of which anthropology is a subset—a regional ontology of one particular form of organism—must tread the fine line between the Scylla of reductionism, in which we lose sight of the qualitative distinctions between different forms of life, plant and animal, animal and human, and the Charybdis of isolationism that fails to recognize the properties that all organisms share. In modern biological thinking we commonly find the first of these failings; in contemporary philosophy, especially but by no means exclusively in its existentialist variety, more often the second. Jonas's chosen tools, phenomenological description and critical analysis, allow him to avoid both perils in an achieved philosophy of life whose conceptual center is the theory of the organism, from whose innate potential properties the manifold variety of life arises in the course of evolution.

Jonas's account of the organism is bold and unusual in attributing, even to its most primitive forms, the germ of properties that normally we recognize only in its higher, more differentiated and chronologically more recent types. Of course, such a notion would not have been strange to Aristotle, to whom all existing being is the actualization of innate potencies of eternally preexistent forms. What is remarkable about Jonas's version of a similar idea is the way in which he shows it to be implicit in the teachings of a theory of process, Darwinian evolution, from which all reference to constancy of form, still more to eternity, has been apparently removed. By reflecting philosophically on that theory, and on the living world it purports generatively to explain, Jonas redeems the essential truth embodied in the Aristotelian view. What is restored is not a universe of unchanging essences and static forms, each qualitatively distinct from the other, but a view of relative constancies and intrinsically necessary conditions of survival that is consonant with the modern scientific conception of nature.

If in describing this world we have recourse to language that recalls the Aristotelian metaphysics of potency and act, this is a function of the degree to which, though innocent of any theory of evolution, Aristotle was a keen observer and analyst of the way the world happened to be and still in large part is. Not the least keen of his observations is his account of man as a form of organic being— a rational and political animal, but an animal nonetheless, distinguished from his fellows by his capacity to reflect upon his fate, and so to choose whatever path might seem most desirable to follow. Through reason, man determines the extent and limit of his possibilities. Through politics, he constructs a second nature, a *polis,* in which he can not only live but thrive.

Jonas, of course, is not Aristotle, nor even, in the strictest sense of the term, like some, a neo-Aristotelian thinker of a recognizably modern type. The philosophical influences on his work are, first, that of Heidegger, and then, in the form of his ethics if not its content, of Kant. And yet our continual invocations of the exemplary significance of Aristotle for Jonas, not least in the range of his philosophy, his rationality, and his attention to empirical, scientific evidence, are hardly accidental—and nowhere more so than in the sphere of his philosophical biology and his stress on the specificity of organic being. Jonas himself refers to Aristotle's *De Anima* as the first philosophical biology, and when we consider the central place of that work in the corpus of Aristotelian writings, as the point at which the works of theoretical reason, the *Physics* and the *Metaphysics,* open out onto the practical philosophy of the *Ethics* and the *Politics,* it is hard to avoid recognizing what might be termed an elective affinity between Aristotle's thought and that of Jonas. For both, it is a philosophy of the organism, and of man as a distinct form of organic being, that provides the point of transition from questions of pure theory to matters of practice.

Needless to say, Jonas's conception of science is hardly Aristotle's. For if anything in Aristotle is untenable today, it is his natural scientific understanding of the universe as a complex of essentially unchanging substances—a view so far removed from our current conception of the world in terms of ceaseless process. And yet, as we have seen, in Jonas's reading of the significance of Darwinian evolution, the historical process of life itself, something still valid in this Aristotelian view is indeed recovered from the darkness into which it had been thrust by the triumph of Cartesian dualism. In Jonas's reading of Darwinism there, above all, it is an Aristotelian conception of the unity of organic being that is redeemed and, with it, the relevance of that unity to our appreciation of the condition of man. For Jonas, as for Aristotle, it is in constitutive features of the organism that the root of our understanding of the possibilities of man is to be found, and, at the same time, it is in the organism we find prefigured the dimensions of dynamic existence that achieve, in man, their fullest expression. Central to this is the phenomenon of freedom and the risks to continuing survival that this entails.

This brings us to the final theme of this chapter, Jonas's complex yet necessary account of organic being in terms of its freedom with regard to the material of which it is composed, and of metabolism as the process by which, through the constant ingestion of material, the organism maintains itself in being. For according to Jonas, metabolism is the unifying mark of life itself, and, as such, the specific difference that essentially distinguishes animate from inanimate matter.

Metabolism, Jonas claims, is the first form of ontological freedom and, by the same token, the unifying specific difference of life. In what, then, does its distinction consist? Only when we have answered this question will we understand how this elementary form of freedom can be said to prefigure, albeit remotely, the multiform freedom of man. It is this that Jonas discusses in "Is God a Mathematician?" (*PL*, 75). And he does so in this context because it is precisely in the tendency of post-Cartesian philosophy and science to understand animate as well as inanimate being in terms of measurable quantity alone—Descartes's *res extensa*—that he perceives its ontological inadequacy as an account of the phenomenon of life.

Of course, the organism, any organism, is like every other physical body in possessing a measurable extended mass, and "As a physical body the organism will exhibit the same general features as do other aggregates: a void mostly, crisscrossed by the geometry of forces that emanate from the insular foci of localized elementary being. But special goings-on will be discernible, both inside and outside its so-called boundary, which will render its phenomenal unity still more problematical than that of ordinary bodies, and will efface almost entirely its material identity through time. I refer to its *metabolism*, its exchange of matter with its surroundings. In this remarkable mode of being, the material parts of which the organism consists at a given instant are to the penetrating observer only temporary, passing contents whose joint material identity does not coincide with the whole which they enter and leave, and which sustains its own identity by the very act of foreign matter passing through its spatial system, the living *form*. It is never the same materially and yet persists as its same self, by not remaining the same matter. Once it really becomes the same with the sameness of its material contents . . . it ceases to live; it dies (or becomes dormant as do certain seeds and spores whose life process stops, to be resumed under appropriate conditions)" (*PL*, 75-76).

In an extended footnote to this passage, Jonas emphasizes the pervasiveness of metabolism within the living system and, at the same time, the inadequacy of seeing in this process only a variant form of the inflow and outflow of materials that, for example, allows a fueled machine, like the engine of a car, to continue to operate. In the organism, "The exchange of matter with the environment is not a peripheral activity engaged in by a persistent core: it is the total mode of continuity (self-continuation) of the subject of life itself. The metaphor of 'inflow and outflow' does not render the radical nature of the fact. In an engine we have inflow of fuel and outflow of waste products, but the machine parts themselves that give passage to this flow do not participate in it: their substance is not involved in the transformations which the fuel undergoes in its passage through them; their physical identity is clearly a matter apart, affected neither by those interchanges nor by their ensuing action. Thus the machine persists as a self-identical inert system over against the changing matter with which it is 'fed'; and, we may add, it exists as just the same when there is no feeding at all: it is then the same machine at a standstill. On the other hand, when we call a living body a 'metabolizing system,' we must include in the term that the system itself is wholly and continuously a result of its metabolizing activity, and further that none of the 'result' ceases to be an object of metabolism while it is also an agent of it" (*PL*, 76).

It is just this distinction between an organism and a machine that

Descartes failed to see; from this failure flows his inability, or un-willingness, to recognize the unifying distinctiveness of living be-ing, of animate as opposed to inanimate nature. This is vital because the identity of the organism, unlike that of the inert physical body, is essentially independent of the sameness of the material of which it is composed. More than this, its continuing identity, its persisting form as living as opposed to dead matter, depends precisely on the ceaseless change of material content achieved through metabolism. It is just this feature that Jonas describes as the innate freedom of the organism with regard to its material substance, on whose un-ending metabolic passage it nonetheless depends but with which it is never identical. And though this is very far from the sense of free-dom that we associate with human existence, yet there too, in the relationship between man and his sustaining environment, we rec-ognize the copresence of nonidentity and dependence that is a uni-versal feature of the phenomenon of life.

In the elementary freedom of the organism with regard to its com-positional substance, Jonas therefore perceives not just the evolu-tionary source, but the ontological germ from which, by way of the successive emerging forms of plant and animal life, the adventure of human existence develops in a process in which every gain in free-dom is accompanied by increasing risk that the adventure of life will not in fact succeed. No form of being is more secure than inert mat-ter and none less than that of man in whom the phenomenon of autonomous being, though never complete, achieves its highest earthly form. It is to this state of being that now we can turn our gaze and so return, gratefully perhaps, to rather less complex or at least to more familiar ground.

Anthropology and the Identity of Man

In an essay on Heideggerian existentialism, Leo Strauss, like Jonas a Jewish student of Heidegger, writes tellingly of the impact that Heidegger had upon the philosophical culture of his time. Strauss was a young Ph.D. when, in 1922, he first heard Heidegger lecture: "Up to that time," he writes, "I had been particularly impressed, as many of my contemporaries in Germany were, by Max Weber: by his intransigent devotion to intellectual honesty, by his passionate devotion to the idea of science—a devotion that was combined with a profound uneasiness regarding the meaning of science. On my way north from Freiburg, where Heidegger then taught, I saw, in Frankfurt-am-Main, Franz Rosenszweig. . . . [A]nd I told him about Heidegger. I said to him that, in comparison with Heidegger, Weber appeared to me as an 'orphan child' in regard to precision and probing and competence. I had never seen before such seriousness, profundity, and concentration in the interpretation of philosophic texts. I had heard Heidegger's interpretation of certain sections in Aristotle, and some time later I heard Werner Jaeger in Berlin interpret the same texts. Charity compels me to limit my comparison to the remark that there was no comparison. Gradually the breadth of the revolution of thought which Heidegger was preparing dawned upon me and my generation. We saw with our own eyes that there had been no such phenomenon in the world since Hegel. He succeeded in a very short time in dethroning the established schools of philosophy in Germany. . . . The same effect which Heidegger produced in the late twenties and the early thirties in Germany, he produced very soon in continental Europe as a whole. . . . All rational liberal philosophic positions have lost their significance and power. One may deplore this, but I for one cannot bring myself to clinging [*sic*] to philosophic positions which have been shown to be inadequate. . . . Only a great thinker could help us in our intellectual plight. But here is the great trouble: the only great thinker in our time is Heidegger."

I cite Strauss's words because today, in a cultural climate dominated, even in Britain and America, by the anarchic and ethically nihilist currents of postmodernism and deconstructionism, which are themselves consequences of the revolution that Heidegger wrought in philosophy, what he says seems even more true than when he wrote it some decades ago. David Cooper has observed that much of Heidegger's fascination lies in "his blending of large philosophical issues with cultural critique," but, to at least so far as those who, like Jonas, felt his immediate impact as a teacher, or who read him with care today, there is rather more to the story than that.

There are of course those who remain resistant to Heidegger's fatal charms. And they can point, easily enough, to acres of text in which Heidegger seems not so much to be wrongheaded as to mean nothing very much at all. Many analytical philosophers, for example, are inclined to see Heideggerian philosophy as exemplifying simply an indulgent misuse of language, a confection of vapid posturings that a good dose of conceptual clarification could conjure away. Unfortunately, not only is it difficult to dismiss all of Heidegger's writings in this way—some are of exemplary clarity and rhetorical power—but the sort of philosophy practiced by those who find nothing of cognitive consequence in Heidegger tends, with rare exceptions, to be confined to purely technical questions of linguistic analysis that have no resonance beyond the rarified circles of an academy in which philosophy itself no longer occupies a central position.

Even when ill done, as all too frequently it is, it is usually only the discourse of theorists influenced in one way or another by Heidegger that penetrates beyond the academy walls to influence the course of current political, social, and scientific debate. And this is so because, whatever the obscurities or oddities of what such theorists seem to say, at least they are recognized to be speaking about matters of general concern. The great impact of a thinker like Michel Foucault on such matters as penal policy and educational practice exemplifies just what this may mean. Whatever we might like, the influence of Heidegger just cannot be wished away, and if that influence is not to leave us simply in a state of moral and cognitive confusion devoid of rational response, we must begin by recognizing that there is much more to the Heideggerian revolution than the jargonizing guff that he bequeathed to his least-talented disciples.

Thinkers as considerable as Strauss or Jonas, not to mention the others I have cited before, were not bowled over by the empty vaporings of a posturing mystagogue. If, in Heidegger, they perceived the authentic voice of a philosophical intelligence uniquely attuned to the dimensions of a civilizational crisis that, a generation before, Nietzsche had called the "nihilism that is knocking at our door," it was because in his teaching they found, not solutions to the problems of the time, but an awareness of what was at stake and a profoundly moving conviction, only with deep reluctance abandoned by Heidegger himself, that philosophical reason was the most potent resource we possess in seeking to respond to the dilemmas of our age. Much of what now passes for theory, irrationalist and antiscientific as it is, is the fruit of that abandonment. The work of Jonas is, by contrast, a rational response to Heidegger's challenge from within its orbit.

Nowhere is this more true than in the field of philosophical anthropology, the theory of the nature and condition of man to which Max Scheler devoted his final years and that he defined, in classic terms in 1924 in "Man and History," as "a basic science which investigates the *essence* and essential constitution of man, his relationship to the realms of nature (organic, plant and animal life) as well as the source of all things, man's metaphysical origin as well as his physical, cultural and social evolution along with their essential capabilities and realities."

Heidegger himself did not altogether dismiss the value of such a grand and grandiose undertaking. However, he believed it to be impossible to fulfill, and he argued powerfully and persistently that all claims to achieve it—by Scheler himself and later by Plessner in *The Stages of Organic Life and Man* and Arnold Gehlen in *Man: His Nature and Place in the World* (1940)—rested upon a failure to attend adequately to the fundamentally elusive nature of man's being in the world and the degree to which all empirical scientific accounts of that nature were at best derivative reflections of fragmentary moments of a process inexhaustible and ultimately impenetrable to reason. This process he called "The History of Being," on whose outcome we can do no more than attend in a spirit of anxious expectation. It was from this state that, in his later interview with *Der Spiegel,* Heidegger famously declared: "Only a god can save us."

This may be taken by some as an expression of hope, but for the philosopher, reliant as he is on the use of his reason and the utilization of available knowledge, it must seem a counsel of despair. Certainly, so far as philosophy goes, it represents a radical denial of the possibility that the philosopher can, through the rational integration of available evidence, succeed in providing his contemporaries with valid, positive insights into the dilemmas that they face and how they may be overcome. Small wonder then that even when the voice of the post-Heideggerian philosopher is, in contrast to that of his less ambitious analytic colleague, heard beyond the confines of academic dispute, it must appear—in comparison with that of the natural scientist, the technocrat, or the man of affairs—eccentric or just quirky, lacking in objective significance and not a little pretentious to a public concerned, naturally enough, with concrete results and practical recommendations. The situation is still worse when, as is often the case, the voice in question is either almost unintelligible, because couched in a jargon unknown to common usage, or, where understood at all, morally disconcerting in its politically reckless endorsement of ethical nihilism or, in its conservative variant, its adoption of a tone of regretful but resigned and passive despair.

"Philosophy," Heidegger observes, "makes nothing happen"; but that is at best a half-truth whose apparent meaning should be neither too readily nor too complacently assumed. Certainly the act of philosophizing, the practice of meditation, or even the exercise of debate is of itself without consequence. Certainly too, if the central task of philosophy is conceived as to say what is—the role of ontology or metaphysics as traditionally conceived—then the act of description and analysis cannot, unlike what the observations of quantum physics are said to do, be admitted to alter by one iota the content of what is described. But nor does such a description leave unaltered the mind in which it occurs, and so the other side of "Philosophy makes nothing happen" must be the recognition that, as the title of Richard Weaver's most famous book avers, "Ideas have consequences." People act on their ideas about the world, and through their actions more or less substantial changes are brought about. Even the most passive of mental responses are, in this roundabout way, contributory to change, and even the most apparently abstract of philosophical notions may be fraught with consequence. It is this that is recognized in the proverb that tells us, "All that is required for evil to triumph is for good men to do nothing."

Thus a philosophy of resignation or despair that induces passivity alone leaves the way open to the free passage of processes brought

about by the actions of others less readily if less thoughtfully resigned to their fate. A philosophy such as that of the later Heidegger, which seems to deny the philosopher the capacity for understanding and rationally intervening in the history of Being, disables
philosophy itself, but in doing so it leaves the field open to the interventions of others less philosophically educated or inclined.
Technologists, politicians, and other practical men will continue to
act, as act they must, without recourse to the teachings of philosophy, and such actions will consequently be less rationally informed
than otherwise they might have been.

In an essay, the eighth in *The Phenomenon of Life,* Jonas considers
what he calls "The Practical Uses of Theory"; there, he observes that
"It is in this realm of concrete judgement and choice that the practical use of theory comes about. Whence it follows that the use of
theory does not itself permit of a theory: if it is enlightened use, it
receives its light from deliberation, which may or may not enjoy the
benefits of good sense. But this knowledge of use is different not
only from the knowledge of the theory used in the case but from that
of any theory whatsoever, and it is acquired or learned in ways different from those of theory. This is the reason why Aristotle denied
there being a science of politics and practical ethics" (*PL,* 199).

This is important when we consider the status of Jonas's philosophical anthropology, which, though primarily descriptive, analytical, and therefore theoretical, is informed, as Heidegger's ontology of *Dasein* is not, by reflective appropriation of and deliberation
on the natural and cultural sciences of man—biology as well as history—and so can be a source of guidance for concrete action and
choice, the realm of practice. What is more, and again in contrast to
Heideggerian teaching, whether of the early decisionist variety of
the thirties or the later meditative slant of passive expectation, still
less the do-as-you-will ethics of postmodernism, the connection between the realms of theory and practice is itself rational. Of itself,
philosophical anthropology makes nothing happen, but insofar as
its informative content—its account of human nature and its conditions of well-being—is rationally comprehensible, it provides the
warrant for deciding rationally upon the choices we should make.
Ethics, as Aristotle taught, is not a theory but a practice; within the
sphere of ethical choice and judgment, one directional decision will
be more rationally justifiable than another, always supposing, as

Jonas will argue we must in the nature of life suppose, that continuation in being is preferable to extinction.

It is here that we see the implication of Jonas's account of the metabolic activity of the organism for our considerations. Unlike inert matter, subject as it is to the slow but remorseless process of physical entropy in consequence of the operation of Newton's—or should we say nature's—laws of thermodynamics, the organism, however primitive, strives, not consciously but purposefully nonetheless, to maintain itself in being. Metabolism is the first, most universal form of this activity, the property of bacterial, plant, and animal being alike. In the case of many animals, this process is supplemented by motility and perception, the reaching toward and grasping of the means of sustenance; in the human, these novel, ontologically unprecedented, dimensions of activity are supplemented by a further range of actions, some of which will, at the limit, be undertaken or not as a consequence of reflective deliberation. This orientation to survival is the teleological property of life that links, across each successive level, the fact of metabolism with the deliberations of ethics. The mode of operation differs in each case, but the governing principle, survival in the face of potential nonexistence, is quite the same. And in every case, what is involved is a process that defies the entropic dynamism of purely physical matter. That all such efforts end individually in defeat—no living being is immortal—is clear enough; but no less clear is the unifying struggle of every animate being to defer that certain end.

Yes, in one sense, Heidegger is correct in characterizing man's existence as a being-toward-death, but such a characterization neither is the exclusive feature of human *Dasein* nor does it even begin to exhaust the structural dynamic that inheres in the phenomenon of life itself. And though human beings are, so far as we know, unique in being aware of their impending oblivion and are therefore alone in being able to determine the priorities of their lives accordingly, it is surely a little eccentric to suppose that the principle governing purpose of such reflections is, always and everywhere, to order existence with a view to what will end them all.

If this were so, it is hard to imagine why court jesters were ever employed, as reputedly they were, to remind their royal masters that they too were destined to die. Such grim reminders ought, in Heidegger's eyes, to have been redundant. They can scarcely have been

a required part of the jester's job description as just another pleas-
ing diversion or joke calculated to raise a smile. Rather, monarchs,
like most of their subjects, were, from day to day, concerned with
other matters than their approaching ends. And who will say, as Heidegger seems to imply, that lives so lived were in any way less authentic than those of the few morbid souls preoccupied from day to
day with the indisputable and inescapable fact that someday they
too would die? Such folk are rare in any age and, if the testaments
of concentration camp survivors are to be believed, unusual even
among those whose settled death was most immediately in hand.
Here it is well to recall that Jonas was a Jewish philosopher and that
the abiding motto of Judaism is "Choose life."

Memento mori, the discipline of Stoics and Christians alike, is a
fine enough exercise, ennobling in its way and even necessary at
times, but it is not the sum, nor even the most remarkable feature of
the *ars vitae.* The art of life is something more than the process of
learning how to die; and before we allow this latter theme to preoc-
cupy our minds, as sometime it most properly will, we can and do
attend to other matters that seem to us at least no less important at
the time. Such matters, in the form of our achievements, cultural and
social, symphonies as well as friendships—whether, like a piece of
written music, enduring in lasting form or, like a relationship, recalled in the memory of our surviving fellows alone—are, far more
than the manner of our dying, the ways in which we who are not
martyrs are best remembered. Even Plato, preoccupied as he was
with the death of Socrates, and to whom we owe the first known
statement of the idea that the well-lived life is the practice of dying,
would not have supposed anything different—or else, instead of
composing his dialogues, he would have sought martyrdom himself.

The worth of the life of Aeschylus, a veteran of Marathon and so,
like Jonas, a proud ex-soldier and, more significantly, the first trage-
dian of the West—the archetypal poet of destined, implacable death
and thus, in some sense, an unsuspecting precursor of Heidegger's
existentialism—lies in the tragedies that survive him and not in the
grimly comic circumstances that brought about his own death. This
came about quite unexpectedly as the result of a tortoise being
dropped on the poet's head from some great height by an eagle seeking to gorge itself on the flesh uncovered within the reptile's shell
once it was broken.

There, in his highest form, man met with another's metabolism in one absurd accidental variant upon the universal fate of life. Such was the *Dasein,* the temporal historical situation, that ended the life of Aeschylus—not implacable destiny to be pondered on, but sheer accident in one of its more outrageously unforeseeable forms. Indeed, if Aeschylus had in his tragedies depicted deaths such as his own rather than the bloody sequence of family murders that is the *Oresteia,* we should see in him the precursor not of the Eliot of *Murder in the Cathedral* but of the surreal, absurdist comedy of death as pictured in Joe Orton's *Loot.* Was such a life as that of Aeschylus, or such a death, in any way inauthentic? To suppose it so is to misconstrue the significance of the phenomenon of life—its underlying unity and the rich manifold of the forms that it may perchance achieve. Which brings us, neatly enough, to the way in which, in "Change and Permanence: On the Possibility of Understanding History," Jonas introduces his most brilliant discussion of philosophical anthropology and the identity of man—by reference not to the Aeschylean tragedies but to their yet more ancient Hellenic forebears, the epics of Homer.

Here are Jonas's opening sentences: "Achilles sulks in his tent, mourns for Patroclus, drags Hector's corpse around the funeral pyre, weeps at Priam's words. Do we understand this? Surely, we do, without being Achilles ourselves, ever having loved a Patroclus and dragged a Hector through the dust. Socrates passed a life in discourse, examines opinions, asks what virtue and knowledge are, makes himself the gadfly of Athens in obedience to the god's command and dies for it. Do we understand this? Yes, we do, without ourselves being capable of such a life and such a death. A wandering preacher calls to two fishermen: Follow me, I shall make you fishers of men; and they leave their nets never to return. Even this we understand, although the like of it has never happened to us, and none of us is likely to follow such a call. Thus do we understand the never experienced from the words of ancient writings" (*PE,* 237).

I spoke before of Jonas as having a style that a novelist and even a poet might envy. Here, if anywhere, we hear something of the poetic quality to which his prose can rise. It is a quality deployed when the case seems to require it, withheld when it does not, and thus, in sum, the poetry of a philosopher is concerned, first and last, with conveying cognitive meaning and not with achieving aesthetic effect. The beauty of the cadences, the nobility of the references are such that an eighteenth-century Augustan might have prized, yet nothing in the manner or matter of what Jonas says is redundant to his philosophic purpose. This is clarification of matters of philosophical anthropology and, as the reference to the possibility of understanding history suggests, the form of knowledge that it provides.

Jonas notes that although, in the cases indicated—Achilles, Socrates, and the Gospel tale—we understand quasi-intuitively what is involved, the question "Do we understand it correctly?" remains unanswered. Can we say, as Leo Strauss maintains in his debate over the nature of hermeneutic understanding with Gadamer, that a historian can and should seek to understand his human object as that past human being understood himself, or, rather, do we depend upon what Gadamer, more deeply influenced here by Heidegger, calls "the fusion of historical horizons" between the world and likely worldview of the interpreter and that of the interpreted, both human beings but each the product of his own historically specific situation? This is a major question in the philosophy of the cultural and social sciences, the *Geisteswissenschaften,* and on its answer depends the sort of knowledge that these sciences can provide.

Jonas's answer is, at first sight, somewhat closer to that of Strauss than to Gadamer's; though here we should note that in *Truth and Method* Gadamer mentions, almost in passing, that the theory of interpretation he advances assumes as its own premise the ontology of transhistorical human constancy established in the anthropological theories of such philosophers as Scheler, Plessner, and Gehlen. For his part, Jonas observes that there are three logical possibilities that underlie the problem of the understanding of the expressions and actions of one man by another from whom he is distanced by time and place. The first is based on the claim, enshrined in the classical view of the essential identity of human nature through time, that man has a nature that is identical in all times and places and that therefore the full range of human experience and response is comprehensible to a cognate human interpreter, who, by virtue of his participation in a shared humanity, can imaginatively reproduce in himself the experience of any other.

Against this must be set the more modern, existentialist view that "*what* man is at any time is the product of his own *de facto* existing and of the choices made therein; and further, that the scope of his existing, even the kind and content of the choices open to it are, in their turn, predetermined by the facticity of spatio-temporal place, by the circumstance and accident of the situation; and, finally, that each such situation is unique" (*PE*, 238–39). Both of these views, Jonas claims, are somewhat too exclusively one-sided. The first requires us to ignore the reality and hermeneutic significance of historical change with all that it implies. The second leads to a radical historical skepticism that seems to suggest that the quest to understand the historical other is doomed to disappointment because, as products of a radically different set of circumstances, we cannot hope truly to comprehend how others lived and felt. Strangely, both these apparently opposing arguments share the view that understanding is necessarily "a 'knowing of the like,' with the difference that in the one case this means the possible truth, and in the other, the necessary error of historical understanding" (*PE*, 239). In the first view we find the inclination to the trite assumption that there is nothing new under the sun; in the second, the counterintuitive implication that every impression of understanding is based upon a misconception of a nonexistent ontological identity of essence.

Neither view is wholly adequate for explaining the truth that while understanding is indeed possible, every such understanding contains within itself the possibility of historical error based on the fact that certain existential possibilities, once extant, are no longer imaginable to the interpreter. And yet, as Jonas observes, these two positions—constancy of human essence and radical historical discontinuity—are not of equal import, for even those who, like Sartre, deny the essential constancy of human nature "predicate their negation . . . not of an empty arbitrary x but of Man, as something attributable to him uniquely and in distinction to the animal, which is captive in each instance to its specific essence; this very negativity thus is claimed for man as an 'essential' property" (*PE*, 240). Therefore what is required is a third position that, while accepting the specific endurance of certain persisting features of humanity, also admits the significance of historical change and the emergence of novelty that this entails. I shall cite in full the passage in which Jonas discusses the merits of all three positions and, in doing so, repeat two pages that appeared originally in my own first book, *Real-*

ism (Manchester: Carcanet Press, 1981). To those who know that work, I apologize while observing that the repetition of what seems still essentially true is never without merit.

"The doctrine of the one, permanent human nature contains the truth that an inalienable kinship links the children of man across the farthest distances of history and the greatest diversities of culture; that this common ground supports and holds together and explains all the manifoldness which unpredictably comes forth from it; and that only with this as a basis is history possible at all, as well as the understanding of it. The doctrine of man's fundamental mutability and actual changing, and of the uniqueness of each product of change, contains the truth that the particularization of humanity in the different cultures, and again in the progress of each culture, and again in the individuals sharing it, produces genuine and unpredictable otherness; that consequently the 'knowledge of like by like' must transcend itself; and that—taking off from the basis of the like—an understanding of the widely different is possible and must be striven for. *How* it is possible, is as yet an open question. Finally, the doctrine of the necessary failure of all understanding contains the truth that the interpreter indeed imports himself into the interpreted, inevitably alienating it from itself and assimilating it to his *own* being and also, that every advance leaves an indelible remainder which recedes before it into infinity" (*PE,* 242–43).

This passage clears the way for Jonas's discussion of the nature of human understanding and historical understanding in particular. Throughout, he stresses the outward-facing nature of consciousness, arguing that we must reject the Cartesian perspective according to which we achieve knowledge of other minds only by analogical inference from consciousness of self. If anything the reverse is true. Knowledge of our own minds, even consciousness of mind as such, is "a function of acquaintance with other minds. Knowledge of inwardness as such, whether one's own or that of others, is based on communication with a whole environment which determines, certainly codetermines decisively, even what will be found in eventual introspection. Since we begin life as infants (a fact philosophers so easily forget), coming into a world already peopled with adults, the particular 'I' to-be is at first far more the receiver than the giver in this communication. In the course of it, the rudimentary inwardness that is 'I' evolves by gradually beholding from the address, utterance and conduct of others what inward possibilities there are and making them its own" (*PE,* 244).

Animal life is expressive and its expressions are directly given to perception. That this extends beyond the range of the human is clear to anyone who has ever seen devotion or fear on the face of a dog; but within humanity its range is greater and its content more highly differentiated. We understand others not because we have any sort of "hot line" to another's consciousness, nor, usually, by analogy with our own experiences, for often we understand that which we have never actually experienced. Understanding rests far more on sensed potentiality for a certain humanly possible experience than on actual experience itself: "To 'know love by love' is not to infer, from my own experience of the feeling of love, what is probably going on in someone else. I may first be awakened by *Romeo and Juliet* to the potentialities of love, by the tale of Thermopylae to the beauty of sacrificial heroism. This is itself an experience, showing me undreamt-of possibilities of my own soul—or rather, of 'the soul'—possibilities that may or may not become actualities of my own experience. *This experience of the potential, mediated by symbols, is precisely what is meant by 'understanding.'* . . . The knowledge of other minds thus rests on the ground of the common humanity of man—in such a manner, however, that the common ground is effective, not by supplying parallels between what *is there* in the self and the other, but by allowing the voice of the other to call on the possibilities that lie latent in the soul or can be elicited from his nature" (*PE,* 246–47).

Jonas then analyzes what he means by the common humanity of man. In the first place, there are the biological constants that are so taken for granted that they are rarely mentioned in explanation. These are the needs of the body for food, water, and sleep, the succession of childhood, adulthood, and old age, the mortality of the body and the duality of the sexes. To recognize the importance of these normally unspoken assumptions, we need only consider the difficulty of explaining Napoleon's retreat from Moscow to a being from another planet who might receive sustenance directly from the atmosphere, fly effortlessly through the air without artificial aids, and require nor more than three hours' sleep a year. A history teacher summoned to teach the rudiments of earth history to the offspring of such a being would soon realize the extent to which these biological constants are assumed in everything he has hitherto said. But the field of constancy is certainly not exhausted at this level.

Passing from the biological to the cultural level, we find the products of man to be just as revealing of the community of human nature. Discovered human artifacts belong to three categories typified respectively by the tool, the image, and the tomb. These categories, Jonas argues, primevally foreshadow the later development of physics, art, and metaphysics. Tool, image, and tomb each points in its fashion to constancy in the nature of man's relationship to the world: "The *tool* (any utensil, including weapon and vessel) tells us that here a being, compelled by his needs to deal with matter, serves these needs in artificially mediated ways originating from invention and open to further invention. The *image* tells us that here a being, using tools on matter for an immaterial end, represents to himself the contents of his perception, plays with their variations and augments them by new shapes—thus generating another object-world of representation beyond the physical objects of his need and its direct satisfaction. The *tomb* tells us that here a being, subject to mortality, meditates on life and death, defies appearance and elevates his thought to the invisible—putting tool and image to the service of such thoughts. These are basic forms in which man, in uniquely human fashion, answers and transcends what is an unconditional given for man and animal alike. With the tool he surpasses physical necessity through invention; with the image, passive perception through representation and imagination; with the tomb, inescapable death through faith and piety. All three, in their transcending function, are divergent modes of a freedom shared by us with the bygone makers of those artifacts and all who came between them and us; so shared, they can serve as universal 'coordinates' of understanding valid for the whole of human history" (*PE*, 252).

Up to this point we have not mentioned language, perhaps the most important thing that distinguishes humankind from the rest of the animal kingdom and without which the other unique traits of humanity could never come to be. The language of another human being, as spoken and written, is potentially understandable both as expressive of man and significative of the world he inhabits. Thus the understanding of an alien language rests, beyond any immediate linguistic affinities it may have with our own, on the constancies of the nature of man and of the surrounding reality in which he participates. But language does more than express the constant elements in the human condition; it is also, as Jonas reminds us, the vehicle of historicity and the medium through which, above the base ground of our common humanity, the unique historical existence of each culture is constituted over time through shared activity and creative innovation.

Within language we find, "on the one hand, the almost secret primordial words or coded insights, in which a particular culture from the outset articulates its posture toward the world, its basic grasp of reality that preconditions all the rest—what we may call the animating spirit of a universe of speech which opens up, and at the same time delimits, its possible range of truth; and, on the other hand, the peaks of poetry and speculation, in which this primordial life of the words comes to its highest (but still deceptive) lucidity of symbolic expression" (*PE,* 257-58). These, the highest and the lowest reaches of language, are to Jonas the most historical of phenomena and therefore those most difficult to understand. Employing the terminology of Voegelin, we may say that the most compact of symbols and the most differentiated of concepts are, of all human expressions, those hardest to access. The wealth of meaning they potentially convey bursts the seams of even the most sensitive interpretation and puts brute certainty to flight.

This is the penumbra of skepticism that attends even the most informed and discriminating of human scientific inquiries and makes of hermeneutic inquiry a field, not of certainty or dogma, but of probabilistic deduction. This is, however, no reason to forswear the pursuit of such inquiries nor doubt their cognitive value. The presence of uncertainty within their cognitive scope is not, after all, a feature of them alone. Rather, it pertains to all spheres of human knowledge. No husband knows for certain what his wife was doing in his absence. No physicist knows for sure that the subatomic particles that he presently identifies in a material body are all that will subsequently be found. But, by the same token, this skeptical view prevents neither the husband from believing his wife to be faithful, nor the physicist from assuming his account of the structural properties of the atom to be as adequate as he can thus far attain. Evidential conviction is a function of judgment based on whatever knowledge may be at hand. To demand of it either more or less would be both practically crippling and theoretically absurd.

Nor are such convictions a matter of individual decision alone. Faced with the same body of evidence, any other reasonable man or woman may be expected to come to the same rational, albeit provisional conclusions. At best, such judgments will be subject to the proviso that requires that, in a court of law, a jury should find for the guilt or innocence of a defendant "beyond reasonable doubt." In every field, such verdicts are subject to potential revision in the light of further evidence, but in none is this alone considered sufficient reason for refusing to arrive at a judgment. In view of the practical importance that legal procedures have in every human society, it is hardly surprising that it is in the rhetorical casuistry of law that the best formulations of the principles of evidential proof and secure judgment should be found, and it is these that we apply when, in the field of philosophical anthropology, we judge between different accounts of the nature and condition of man. By this standard, we can hardly avoid the conclusion that Jonas's account, drawing as it does on the multiformity of available evidence, stands up very well indeed.

Ethics and Responsibility
in a Technological Age

This book began with the bold claim that the philosophy of Hans Jonas provides a perspective on the present position and future prospects of mankind that is, in its power and wisdom, unequalled in the work of any of his contemporaries; in succeeding chapters I have shown the way in which his reflections proceed rationally in offering a scientifically informed account of the nature of man's being in the world that recognizes, at once, the material and biological foundations of that being and the unique features that set it apart from all other forms of life. In this chapter, we come to what is, in terms of its general significance, his masterwork, *The Imperative of Responsibility: In Search of an Ethics for the Technological Age* (1984).

Jonas was, as I have indicated, a master of the essay form, and the bulk of his writing consists of essays, some relatively brief and others extended, but each, as Leon Kass observes, "a self-contained little gem—hard, compact, offering many facets of the complex issues discussed." His concentration on the essay form is partly a matter of taste and partly a function of the circumstances of his life. Because of the disruption of his academic career brought about by his exile from Germany, and the fact that, in contrast to other intellectual exiles, he responded by taking up the profession of arms, he was already in his forties when he took up his first academic post. Such a life leaves room enough for reflective thought—indeed, in Jonas's estimation, required it—but it is not conducive to the production of lengthy systematic treatises requiring ready access to the materials of research. Thus it is hardly surprising that only the first of his major works, the study of Gnosis, and the last, *The Imperative of Responsibility*, take the form of monographs.

As I have indicated in my discussion of *The Phenomenon of Life*, this matters less in Jonas's case than it would in that of other thinkers, for his thought is characterized by an enviable capacity to systematically cross the boundaries of individual essays and apparently discrete areas of inquiry. This is why his work evinces a quality of integrity in the dual sense that not only is it profoundly moral in seeking to respond, rightly and rationally, to the troubles of his age, but also that it integrates the diversity of his concerns in a single, unified philosophical project that is both inclusive and coherent. The path that begins with the comparative study of ancient and modern forms of nihilism culminates in the formulation of an ethics for a technological age. The writings are many and varied; the project that guides them is intelligibly one. In its beginning is its end.

We may speak of the intrinsic purposefulness of Jonas's work, its innate teleology; and this is especially apt in characterizing the philosophy of a thinker who, more than any other, restores to the account of nature that feature of teleological organization that vanished from the worldview of natural science with the end of Aristotelian physics and biology in the seventeenth century. I hope that I have said enough about Jonas's philosophical biology, his theory of the organism, to indicate that this retrieval of an understanding of the teleological dimension of organic being requires no sacrifice of the cognitive advances that mark the superiority of modern to ancient science.

Modern science was not wrong to reject the ancient view that every being was purposefully determined to seek its proper place in an innately ordered cosmos. Where it failed was in not recognizing that measurable processes, blind and purposeless in themselves, could nevertheless be structurally organized into forms that secured, if not their permanent endurance, then at least lasting survival as living beings. Such forms required no element of conscious creative design, as the Deists still assumed, nor their individual possession of an innate purposive essence, such as Aristotle supposed. The phenomenon of metabolism, in which foreign material is absorbed into the identity of the animate body, is enough to ensure that even in a world governed only, as Jacques Monod suggests in the title of his famous book, by *Chance and Necessity,* the element of teleology does not entirely disappear. Purposefulness is not a feature of human life alone; it is a common property of animate being that quite unconsciously seeks to survive in living form. And while the Darwinian theory of natural selection, in which only the fittest survive, allowed this ontologically unprecedented property of animate being to be explained without reference to conscious design by providing an account of the mechanism by which novel and more highly differentiated forms of organism, including man, could evolve, it also thereby reestablished the continuity of living forms that the dualism of Descartes had separated into the ontologically unrelated realms of mind and matter—realms that were, for Descartes himself and his immediate successors, mysteriously and uniquely conjoined in the miracle of man. By the same token, the account of evolutionary continuity in the history of life not only permits but even requires us to seek to identify the ways in which the features of each emergent species can be ontologically prefigured, as potential yet to be achieved, in the properties of its ancestors. The origin of life remains itself unexplained and, in Darwinian terms alone, inexplicable, but, once existent, the natural history of life is pregnant with the possibilities of man.

To articulate this is the grand design of Jonas's work. It is the link that binds, in a single chain of argument, the theory of ethics to the philosophy of life. More than this, it is possible to conceive the sum of Jonas's philosophy as a single, uniquely articulate response to the imperative of survival already primitively embodied in the dynamic process of metabolism. There is no element of nature mysticism in this idea. It is based on the observation that the same orientation to self-preservation in living form that governs metabolic activity also explains why one particular twentieth-century thinker should seek, through the processes of mental activity, philosophical reflection and response, to think his way out of the mortal threat to his own continuing existence posed by the challenge of life-destroying nihilism. Insofar as that nihilism was embodied physically in the armies of Nazi Germany, that challenge would have to be met by recourse to equal and, as fortune would have it, superior physical force. But inasmuch as the ideology of Nazism was itself conditioned by a climate of ideas that permitted its emergence, and even made it appear, to Heidegger at least, to provide a life-enhancing purposeful solution to the survival requirements of his race—a means by which the German people, but not Jonas, could secure their historical existence in the face of the challenge of global technology—the challenge could only be met by answering the Heideggerian account of existence with one at once more rational and more humanly inclusive. This is what Jonas sought to accomplish and, in my view, succeeded in doing.

Hans-Georg Gadamer, perhaps the most perceptive because most sympathetic critic of Heidegger's work, speaks of Heidegger's "one way," his single governing path of reflection that guides his life's work in an unbroken sustained attempt to think the question of Being in ever new ways, but always with the intent of seeking to answer the enigmatic challenge of history to his own being. The guiding questions of his thought, late as well as early, are, to use Heidegger's own terms, anchored in the concernful appropriation of whatever possibilities are still available in the historical situation as he perceives it to be. Unfortunately, after the disastrous miscarriage of National Socialism, which proved to be not what Heidegger had first taken it to be, the only form of appropriation turns out to be resigned attendance upon the unforeseeable but hoped-for dispensations of the history of Being to deliver us from the forgetfulness into which we have been cast, potentially fatally, by the realization of metaphysics in the objectified form of the age of world technology. In a quite different way, Jonas, starting from the same premise, pursues, no less implacably, an alternative, single, responsive path that parallels and answers Heidegger's own.

In order to get the full measure of the significance I attach to *The Imperative of Responsibility* and, with it, the basis of my claim, exaggerated as it may seem, for the unequalled importance of Jonas's philosophical work, greater than that of Wittgenstein and more salutary than that of Heidegger, the twin peaks of the contemporary philosophical universe, it is necessary to make a few preliminary clarifying remarks before turning to an examination of the argument of the book. For Jonas is, in comparison with either Wittgenstein or Heidegger, a relatively unknown thinker, especially in Britain and America, and when a commentator makes so bold a claim for such a figure, it will inevitably raise the suspicion that he is endeavoring to build up a cult, a philosophical sect, around the ideas of someone who happens to be his favorite thinker with all the parochial eccentricity which that implies.

I, for one, have no wish to add to the number of such sects, of which there are already quite enough on the intellectual scene, each with its body of hagiographic literature, its more or less academically respectable journal, its regular gatherings at which the faithful may meet to exchange ideas, and now its web sites, too. What Jonas says is too important to become the property of such a group, however admirable its intentions. He needs not to be memorialized but to be introduced to a wider public in order that his work, especially in ethics, can enter into general circulation where it will, when appreciated and understood, serve to counterbalance both the academic confinement of philosophy, which is the regrettable legacy of Wittgenstein, and its deviation into forms of antiscientific irrationalism, which is the major legacy of Heidegger. Only further examination and popularization of the argument of *The Imperative of Responsibility* will allow this to occur and permit us to see him as something more than yet another relatively minor figure in the intellectual firmament, a mere name in the history of twentieth-century thought. But for that to happen I must clarify further what I mean in saying both that Jonas provides an alternative, parallel, and yet opposed path of reflection to that of Heidegger and why the provision of such a path should be so necessary.

And here it is reference to Heidegger, rather than to Wittgenstein or any other supposed master thinker, that is crucial, not only because of the influence that Heidegger has on so many areas of our culture, informing the spirit of a deeply unspiritual age, but because there is a real, identifiable sense in Leo Strauss's claim that "Only a great thinker could help in our intellectual plight," and that our current misfortune is that "the only great thinker in our time is Heidegger."

Note that Strauss says "great thinker," not "great philosopher"; for as a philosopher in a strict sense, Wittgenstein, perhaps Husserl, and maybe others too have as much if not more title to the term *great* as does Heidegger; but their work, in contrast to Heidegger's, has a more narrow cultural reference and import. It serves, in Wittgenstein's case, to cleanse the language of confusions and, in Husserl's, to direct our attention to the ultimate derivation of scientific theories from the data of immediate perception of what he calls the "life-world," *Lebenswelt*—the world as it appears in the uneducated form of natural experience that we share by virtue of our birth of human stock. In neither case, however, does such a work, however estimable and necessary it may be, provide us, as Heidegger's does, with a worldview that encompasses not only our common experience of everyday existence but a powerful understanding of the impact that the expanding influence of global technology has on the quality of that experience and the prospects for that existence. I do not know if Jonas is, in Strauss's sense, a great thinker proportionate to Heidegger—only time will tell. What I do think is that his work provides an equivalent but more rational worldview of just these dimensions.

In *The Imperative of Responsibility,* we find just the measure of these dimensions. First published in Germany in 1979 as *Das Prinzip Verantwortung,* it received an acclaim and achieved a circulation unmatched when, five years later, it appeared in English translation. This, to some extent, was the result of the popularity and prestige that Jonas then enjoyed as a lecturer to foundations and conferences that brought together academics, businessmen, and political leaders in a distinctively if not uniquely German way. The existence of such institutions and events provided a more fertile ground for the book's acceptance than was the case in English-speaking lands, while also ensuring that it reached a wider audience than that of interested university teachers. Then again, the style of philosophy it exemplified, so much broader in scope than the analytical mode fashionable in Britain and hardly less so in the United States, resonated more naturally in continental Europe and ensured that in its pages Jonas's fellow philosophers could recognize a masterly example of their craft and not a trespassing beyond professional boundaries by one who should know better.

In Germany in particular, the subtitle of the book, *In Search of an Ethics for the Technological Age,* seemed to answer a question broached philosophically by Heidegger in 1962 in a widely discussed work translated into English as *The Question Concerning Technology* (1977); in its invocation of the theme of ethics, it promised a perspective on the matter that was notably absent from Heidegger's own discussion of the issue in terms of the fatality of the history of Being— a discussion that in any terms other than Heidegger's own seemed almost exclusively metaphysical and devoid of ethical content. This too contributed to the book's success not simply in Germany, where it sold more than two hundred thousand copies, but, notably, in Italy, where it was awarded the 1992 Premio Nonino for the best book translated into Italian that year.

It would be wrong to say that Jonas's new work passed unnoticed in Britain, but certainly, in comparison with its reception in continental Europe, it seems to have caused little stir even among those ecologically oriented circles to whom it might have been expected to have a special interest and appeal. Nor did the fact that its translation, by Jonas himself in collaboration with David Herr, resulted in an exceptionally eloquent work of English prose seem to make much difference to its British circulation when first it appeared. Perhaps today, when concerns induced by fears of various forms of technological innovation, if not of ethics, are more prevalent in the public mind, the situation may be changing. If so, the time may be ripe for a proper appreciation of a philosophical voice that can bring a much-needed balance to debates in which there is too much confusion and mutual incomprehension between the well-funded but widely distrusted proponents of technological innovation and a public greedy for the material benefits such innovations may bring but dangerously ignorant of the science that underlies them and understandably fearful of where the increasing pace and uncertain direction of change may lead.

Nothing could be more damaging to our prospects than the domination of popular debate by an ill-informed distrust of science as such and an equivalent ignorance among scientists of the genuine ethical concerns that their work inevitably involves when carried over into technological developments that may alter radically the quality and nature of our existence in areas as diverse as reproductive technology and the genetic modification of foods. Unfortunately, despite an abundance of government-funded advisory bodies charged with the sometimes conflicting tasks of providing legislators with expert guidance on matters in which they have little competence and with informing the public of the implications of emergent technologies, a state of confusion seems to prevail among politicians and public alike. Never, perhaps, has there been more need for the balanced voice that only a scientifically literate and ethically sensitive philosophy can provide. It is this that we presently lack and that Jonas can preeminently provide.

Despite the years that have elapsed since its publication, *The Imperative of Responsibility* provides, even today, a framework for debate in which the considerations of ethics, the implications of science, and the interests of a suspicious public can each be given due consideration; it does so because, better than any other work I know, it articulates a clear understanding of just what is novel and what is unchanged about the choices we face in consequence of an ongoing technological revolution of unprecedented speed and scope. The power of modern technology has decisively changed the dimensional range of possible human actions, extending the consequences of our decisions spatially, temporally, and even ontologically into regions that previously lay beyond human interference or control. Consequently, many of our traditional ethical responses, concerned as they were with regulating the proper conduct of people toward one another and with the short-term results of their actions, are quite unable to cope, practically or theoretically, with activities that have an unprecedented causal reach. Responsibility is the correlate of power, and such is our transformative power not only over other men but over the nature on which our survival depends, including our own genetically determined nature as beings capable of exercising ethical choice, that all previous systems of moral belief seem inadequate. This is not because they were necessarily wrong but because they were not designed to cope with the current and prospective scope of human agency.

As John Herz put it at the time of the book's publication, "Traditional ethics has always dealt with individual action within a given space (family, tribe, nation) and a given period (the present, or at most the immediate future); it took the existence of surrounding nature and that of indefinite numbers of succeeding generations for granted. Now everything is changed. An ethics of responsibility must give priority to the maintenance of the possibility of life on earth; it is an ethics of common survival." This requires not abandonment of well-tried forms of ethical reasoning and judgment but the radical revision of our convictions in ways that will take account of the technologically conditioned extension of human agency. Such a reformation can only be effective if undertaken in a spirit of rational appreciation of the intrinsic risks of the course on which we are set. It has become common to appeal to what is called the "precautionary principle" in trying to decide whether or not we should pursue a particular, currently available line of scientific research and seek out its practical applications. Jonas puts matters rather more strongly than that, proposing that we be guided by what, strikingly, he calls a "heuristics of fear."

By this Jonas means that in our pursuit of technological innovation we should educate ourselves to imagine always what may be the worst consequences of what we do; he bases this apparently unbalanced recommendation, formulated in polemical opposition to what the explicitly utopian Marxist theorist, Ernst Bloch, called the "principle of hope," on the recognition that now, no more than ever before, can we hope to foresee the full consequences of what we do, and that, given the unprecedented causal reach of our innovations, we must be aware of the fact that the consequences of our actions are such that the very possibility of human survival may be put at risk. I cannot emphasize too strongly that, contrary to what the apparently apocalyptic overtones of his formulation may suggest, Jonas is anything but an apocalyptic prophet preaching an antiscientific prophecy of despondency and doom. Toward the end of *The Imperative of Responsibility,* he has a passage in which he justifies the bias of his formulation by observing that such a bias is necessary in view of the "heuristics of hope which has hitherto lighted mankind's path" in his pursuit of technological innovation.

He concedes the charge of one-sided emphasis in what he says but denies that this embodies a "bias against technology as such, let alone against science." The "'technological imperative' is nowhere questioned" in what he says, "as it is indeed unquestioned in its anthropological primacy and integral to the human condition. But it needs no advocates in the Western world of the twentieth century: intoxication has taken its place. As things are with us, the technological drive takes care of itself—no less through the pressure of its self-created necessities than through the lure of its promises, the short-term rewards of each step, and not least through its feedback-coupling with the progress of science. There are times when the drive needs moral encouragement. . . ." But "Ours is not one of them. In the headlong rush, the perils of excess become uppermost. This necessitates an ethical emphasis which, we hope, is as temporary as the condition it has to counteract. But," he adds, "there is also a timeless precedence of 'thou shall *not*' over 'thou shalt' in ethics. Warning off from evil has always . . . been more urgent than and peremptory than the positive 'thou shalt' with its disputable concepts of moral perfection. To keep free from guilt comes first in moral duties, the more so when the temptations to guilt become more powerful. Our particular version of this emphasis is in answer to the particular, epochal, perhaps passing phase of civilization and its particular, overpowering temptations. In thus paying tribute to the present state of things, our one-sidedness follows the ancient ethical council of Aristotle that, in the pursuit of virtue as the 'mean' between the two extremes of excess and deficiency, one should fight that fault more which one is more prone to and therefore more likely to commit, and rather lean over in the opposite direction, toward the side less favoured by inclination and circumstances" (*IR*, 203-4).

It is in the Aristotelian perspective of seeing merit in the pursuit of the golden mean that we should understand the primacy that Jonas accords in his ethics to "the heuristics of fear" in an age intoxicated with the dynamism of a largely self-propelling process of technological advance. Such a position, far from representing an anthropological fantasy, reminiscent of the "back to nature" school of Rousseau or, more recently, Ludwig Klages and many but not all of our current Greens, rests upon Jonas's recognition of the intrinsically technological character of man's being in the world. The slogan "back to nature" is only a slogan, not least because the only nature that man has ever been able to inhabit is nature as changed and modified by culture; and culture, even in its most primitive stone age forms, has always made use of and depended on technology, as evidenced by the ubiquitous presence of hand axes among ancient remains uncovered from our prehistoric past by archaeologists.

This means that even the term *technological age,* though apt enough for Jonas's purpose, must be treated with due caution. The technological modification of nonhuman nature is, from the beginning, inscribed in the human form of being in the world. *Homo sapiens* is, by the same token, and at least as originally, *Homo faber;* the use of technology, matter rationally fashioned to a given purpose, is what primordially sets humanity apart from other forms of animal life. For while other animals must adapt to their environment or perish, we survive by adapting the environment to our requirements, whether through the first use of furs and fire to protect us from the cold or in our centrally heated and air-conditioned dwellings from which all impact of the natural climate has been excluded. In this sense, the idea that ours is a distinctively technological age is, while heuristically useful, a somewhat simplistic misconception of a stage in what is a natively human form of being. All ages in which men have existed have been, to some degree, technological; it is in the degree to which technological modification of nature is possible, and not such modification per se, that ours is unique. Technology alone is what makes the continuation of human life possible; and technology becomes questionable only when its development ceases to serve that end. We have now reached this point and must thus cope with its problems. And it is this, Jonas argues, that funda-

mentally alters the relationship between technology and ethics—
what we can and what we ought to do—even though both are innately human dimensions that pertain *ab origine* to our specific form
of life.

Furthermore, even the intrinsic dynamism of technological change
that is such a feature of our present state, is, in itself, nothing new.
While extremely slow in the early stages of human history, it has
tended to increase exponentially over time but is not, any more than
the use of technology itself, a unique feature of contemporary man.
Rather, what is altered today is neither our dependence on technology nor the changing forms it takes, still less the requirement that
we judge how and when any given technology should be used. The
crucial change of which we must take account lies elsewhere—in the
change in the balance between man and the nature brought about
by the cumulative effects of past technological advance. The result
of this is described by Jonas in a memorable passage in which he
characterizes the position we have now achieved and which deserves
to be cited at some length as indicative of his understanding of the
position in which appeal to the heuristics of fear becomes a justifiable and even necessary part of an ethical stance oriented to our future survival.

Today, "the boundary between 'city' and 'nature' has been obliterated: the city of men, once an enclave in the nonhuman world,
spreads over the whole of terrestrial nature and usurps its place. The
difference between the artificial and the natural has vanished, the
natural is swallowed up in the sphere of the artificial, and at the same
time the total artifact (the works of man that have become 'the world'
and as such envelops their makers) generates a 'nature' of its own,
that is, a necessity with which human freedom has to cope in an
entirely new sense. Once it could be said *Fiat justitia, pereat mun-
dus,* 'Let justice be done, and may the whole world perish'—where
'world,' of course, meant the renewable enclave within the imper-
ishable whole. Not even rhetorically can the like be said anymore
when the perishing of the whole through the doings of man—be
they just or unjust—has become a real possibility. Issues never legislated come into the purview of the laws which the total city must
give itself so that there will be a world for the generations of man to
come" (*IR,* 10). From this it follows that the field of ethics, once confined to the ordering of relationships between men, must be ex-

tended to man's dealings with nature as providing the now fragile foundation for his own continued being as a moral agent capable of making decisions.

This, as Jonas notes, adds a new spatial and a new temporal dimension to Kant's moral teaching, whose categorical imperative tells us that we ought to treat other human beings as we would ourselves be treated. As Kant formulates it, the categorical imperative is adequately contained in the injunction: "Act so that you can will that the maxim of your action be made the principle of a universal law." But in the changed circumstances of today's world, this must now be reformulated, more inclusively, as: "Act so that the effects of your action are compatible with the permanence of genuine human life," or, alternatively, "In your present choices include the future wholeness of Man among the objects of your will" (*IR*, 11). The required extension of the spatial dimension lies in its inclusion within the scope of the moral law of the material conditions, the integrity of nature, which alone permits the endurance in being of moral beings, men. The concomitant extension of the temporal dimension is the novel inclusion within the moral calculation of reference to the future effects of action and thereby "the continuance of human agency in times to come" (*IR*, 12).

Thus, while Kant's injunction is essentially private and addressed primarily to the individual in his dealings with other individuals— an ethic of private citizenship—Jonas's reformulation is necessarily collective and political. It is addressed to statesmen, and it requires attention to questions of public policy in which the fate of nature and so of future moral agents can be decided. Here, once again, we note the characteristic combination of innovation and retrieval in Jonas's thought; for, in extending Kant's categorical imperative as he does, Jonas retrieves the political dimension that was, in Aristotle, inseparable from ethics. At the same time, and again in keeping with the Aristotelian tenor of his thought, consideration of moral rectitude is reinserted within a general philosophy of nature of which human nature is an integral part.

This is what I mean when I say that while Jonas's ethical theory is Kantian in form, embodying as it does a reformulation of the categorical imperative that enjoins us to treat human beings as ends to be valued in themselves, it is Aristotelian in content insofar as responsibility toward our fellow men is conceived to be inseparable from our responsibility for stewardship of nature on whose endurance the continuing survival of human, moral agents recognizably depends. In an age of global technology that potentially threatens to undermine the humanly supporting order of nature, only such a recovery of the broader ethical perspective of Aristotelian thought, and of classical thought in general, can be considered adequate to meeting the needs of the time.

Lawrence Vogel, the editor of Jonas's posthumous volume of theological essays, *Mortality and Morality* (1996), calls his overall introductory essay to the collection "Hans Jonas's Exodus," and in it he describes Jonas's philosophy as offering "one of the most systematic and challenging rejoinders to the legacy of Heidegger in particular, and to the spirit of the twentieth century as a whole" (*MM*, 4). The title and the characterization are both apt. "Exodus" invokes not only Jonas's exile from Germany but also his philosophical passage from the nihilistic assumptions of post-Nietzschean German existentialism, exemplified in the teachings of Heidegger, to a philosophical position based on a rational metaphysical account of the phenomenon of life, in whose intrinsic structure he seeks to found a no less rational ethics of responsibility. This ontologically grounded ethics endeavors to show that our sense of what is right and wrong is not a matter of subjective personal preference but an objective property disclosed to reason as inherent in the structure of Being. We do not posit values by an act of will or choice; we discover them as present in the facts of life of which we are an evolutionary product but one in whom, uniquely, the intrinsic rationality and goodness of Being, its worthiness to survive, is disclosed to consciousness.

Jonas's thinking encompasses a theology, to which we will turn in our next chapter, but it is essential to his position that we should recognize that these properties of goodness and rationality are not a function of faith in a supernatural God, envisaged as the author of creation, but are knowable to reason alone. Jonas describes theology as "a luxury of reason," meaning that belief in a beneficent but not, as we shall see, omnipotent deity is compatible with what we know of the structure of the world, and our nature and place within it, but is not required in order to perceive the world as inherently both reasonable and good. The objective validity of an ethics of responsibility is not a teaching of revelation but, according to Jonas, a rational apprehension of the way the world is; and, as Vogel puts it, a "rational metaphysics must be able to ground an imperative of responsibility without recourse to faith" (*MM*, 6).

In this sense, Jonas is a philosophical naturalist though emphatically not a materialist; and thus a thinker more akin to Aristotle than to any of his contemporaries. No more is he an historical idealist in the Hegelian mold, for there is in his philosophy no sense that the process of world history can be understood as a logical or dialectical unfolding of a governing principle culminating in the ever more rational being of man. The process that Jonas describes in *The Phenomenon of Life* is a process of ever increasing differentiation of life forms but one which is governed by contingency alone. It is apprehensible to reason but is not itself a rational process embodying an overall purpose or a rationally intelligible developmental idea. Reason is a contingent feature of man alone, and man is a contingent product of the intelligible but purposeless history of life. The history of life is intelligible as a succession of developmental events, but each of these events is the result of a mutation that is, so far as we can apprehend, a product only of chance. What is intelligible in this process is why some of these events should have produced enduring results in the form of beings capable of survival. What is unintelligible is why any of these events should first have occurred. This is why we must say, apparently paradoxically, that though the history of life is intelligible in terms of evolution, there is no overall intelligibility to an evolutionary process which, while engendering purpose, is not itself inherently purposeful. If, nevertheless, we attribute an overall purpose to this process, that attribution can only be a function not of empirical knowledge but of religious faith that our knowledge of reality may allow but does not logically require. This is why Jonas is so insistent in his separation of the realm of knowledge, including that unfashionable form of knowledge that we call metaphysics, from the realm of faith.

Where he differs from most other contemporary philosophers is not only that he regards metaphysics as a form of knowledge that is independent of faith, a function of rational reflection on the empirically available evidence of nature, but that he sees it as the necessary foundation for an ethics of responsibility capable of guiding us through the dilemmas of our time. One has only to consider what this implies in order to recognize how unusual it must seem in the context of our current postmodernist climate of ideas and how far it seems to fly in the face of the spirit of the age. For if there are any two beliefs that the various divergent forms of postmodernist thought can be said dogmatically to share, they are, first, that metaphysics is obsolete and, second, that ethical choice is a matter of personal preference alone. Both are beliefs that Jonas would lead us to reject. Small wonder then that even a commentator as sympathetic as Lawrence Vogel should "worry that a pluralistic culture cannot bear the burden of such a substantive metaphysics," and that "If our future depends on citizens agreeing with Jonas's speculations, then I fear we are not up to the task" (*MM*, 6). And yet, if Jonas is right, the price we will pay for rejecting his view is, at best, continuing intellectual and moral confusion and, at worst, our extinction as a species. Indeed, given the extent of the powers that technology has put at our disposal and the ease with which they can be employed, the second seems a rather more likely outcome than the first.

At this point we can see how serious a business Jonas takes philosophy to be. A metaphysical philosophy is always a more serious business than one that is metaphysically empty; and a metaphysics that is as devoid of providential reassurance as that of Jonas is perhaps as serious as anyone can conceive. Nor, as we shall see in the next chapter, is there anything in Jonas's theology to which we could look for alternative assurance or consolation, for his is a theology that takes seriously the idea that if God created man, as Jonas believed he did, he created him as a free being endowed with powers that permit him to choose not only his own fate but that of the earth in which he has been set. What man does with his entrusted world is left to him alone, and though Jonas believes in a certain sophisticated, but not sophistical, sense in the immortality of the human soul, about which he writes movingly and persuasively in his essay "Immortality and the Modern Temper" (*MM*, 115–30), there is nothing even in his religious convictions that leads him to suppose that the story of earthly life necessarily ends in success. Quite the reverse, for it is in the nature of life, and not simply of human life, that every evolutionary advance is attained at the cost of increasing risk of individual and collective group extinction.

In the case of man, possession of theoretical and practical reason results in the achievement of a life form quite capable of bringing to an end its own and every other form of life. Equally, however, the same faculties that can bring about universal destruction are, when turned reflectively toward understanding the conditions of survival and well-being, capable of ensuring indefinite if not eternal existence. But this requires of man the exercise of rational choice in an ethics of responsibility and prudential care that encompasses not only human life but the integrity of the nature on which his own depends. The metaphysics that shows this is devoid of appeal to either providence or progress. It is rational but makes no claim to be complete; it begins, modestly enough, with a single, apparently metaphysically innocent, sentence in which Jonas states the grounding principle of his ethics, proceeding deductively from there. The sentence runs: "Man is the only being known to us who can assume responsibility." On which Jonas observes that: "We immediately recognise this 'can' as more than a simply empirical fact. We recognize it as a distinguishing and decisive feature of human existence. Thus, we have in this fact a basic principle of philosophical anthropology, i.e. of the ontology of the being 'Man,' and with it already a principle of metaphysics—but only of the metaphysics of man" (*MM*, 106). Yet from this modest beginning, the rest of metaphysics and, with it, ethics may be said to follow.

Here, in brief, is how the metaphysical deduction proceeds: "We intuitively recognise in this ontological distinction of man—his capacity for responsibility—not only its *essentiality* but also a *value*. The appearance of this value in the world does not simply add another value to the already value-rich landscape of *being* but surpasses all that has gone before with something that generically transcends it. This represents a qualitative intensification of the valuableness of *Being as a whole*, the ultimate object of our responsibility. Thereby, however, the capacity for responsibility as such— besides the fact that it obligates us to exercise it from case to case— becomes *its own object* in that having it obligates us to perpetuate *its presence in the world*. This presence is inexorably linked to the existence of creatures having that capacity. Therefore, the capacity for responsibility per se obligates its respective bearers to make existence possible for future bearers. In order to prevent responsibility from disappearing from the world—so speaks its immanent commandment—there ought to be human beings in the future" (*MM*, 106).

This is, however, only a first step, for what is required in order that the phenomenon of responsibility be sustained is not only the future presence of human beings as such but humans who have not just the ontological capacity for responsibility but also the "psychological openness" to perceive its obligation, and this is "an historically acquired vulnerable possession that can be lost collectively, even if calculative reasoning and power arising from it survive with the biological subjects" (*MM*, 106). This introduces a cultural dimension to the argument, for as Aldous Huxley describes it in *Brave New World,* and B. F. Skinner in *Beyond Freedom and Dignity,* it is possible to conceive of human beings from whom awareness of such an obligation has been removed. In the case of Skinner at least, this may even be regarded as an advantage, and so, even though persuasive, the argument for the persistence of a disposition to act responsibly remains at least debatable—an object of evaluative judgment; and this is why, though persuasive, the argument that Jonas advances falls something short of being a conclusive proof. And here we must, I think, refer back from the argument for human responsibility as such, to Jonas's account of the intrinsic orientation of life to its own preservation in being already primitively foreshadowed or prefigured in the process of metabolism that is a universal feature of animate being. This, I would suggest, demonstrates more potently than anything else the continuity between the philosophy of the organism and Jonas's ontologically grounded ethics, and so the integral unity and rational coherence of his thought.

In an essay on biological engineering, collected in his 1974 anthology of philosophical essays (*PE,* 141-67), Jonas explicitly engages with the ethical problems entailed with the extension of human technological agency into a field, human cloning, that was, when the essay was written, only a possibility dimly foreseen. It is impossible to read that essay today without being struck by the prophetic clarity with which he perceived the issues that such an undertaking would raise and by the emotive yet rational force and discriminating intelligence with which he warns against its pursuit.

Rather than trying to summarize his argument, which is as scientifically informed as it is persuasive but would require a chapter in itself, I shall end this chapter on ethics and technology by citing the final paragraphs of what he has to say in a passage that exemplifies, more topically than anything other, Jonas's contribution to the continuing claims of philosophical reason to be heard in the age of science: "We have been moving for some stretch now at the very boundaries of things human and of possible discourse about them. A spectral sense of unreality must have communicated itself to the reader, which I share. Yet he would be wrong to regard the discourse therefore as otiose. The danger is that we may be gliding into fateful beginnings unawares, innocently as it were by the thin end of the wedge, namely pure science. I have tried, in discussing these borderline cases, to suppress the metaphysical shudder I feel at the idea of a man-made homunculus. To let it out now with an archaic word, the production of human freaks would be an abomination; let alone the unspeakable thought of human-animal hybrids which, quite consistently, has not failed to enter the lists. Steering clear of metaphysics and categories of the sacred, which this topic makes it not easy to do, I resort at the end, and with reference to the whole field of biological control, to the plainest of moral reflections: Deeds with no accountability are wrong when done to others. The moral dilemma in all human-biological manipulation, other than negative. . . . is this: that the potential accusation of the offspring against his makers will find no respondent still answerable for the deed, and no possible redress. Here is a field for crimes with complete impunity to the perpetrator. This alone should call forth the utmost scrupulousness and sensitivity in applying the rising powers of biological control on man. And though much more is involved, the simple ethics of the case are enough to rule out the direct tampering with human genotypes . . . from the very beginning of the road—that is, impalatable as it sounds to modern ears, at the fountainhead of experimental research" (PE, 166–67).

Theological Perspectives

Theology, in the Middle Ages, was described as "the queen of the sciences." Today, she is at best a constitutional monarch, respected and revered by some, but deprived of her once-governing powers over the realm of scientific knowledge. Hans Jonas is, to put it metaphorically, a theorist of theological constitutionalism. Some of his most interesting ideas are to be found in his writings on theology; and, like his ideas in other fields, his theological conjectures form an integral part of a single coherent vision of existence. But they do not control his philosophy of nature, nor decide the content of the science that informs his metaphysical overview of man's nature and place in the cosmos. Following Kant, Jonas describes theology as "a luxury of reason," and, as we have seen, he grounds his imperative of responsibility in a naturalistic metaphysic that judges the continuing existence of the living world, and of man, to be a good in itself apprehensible to reason quite apart from "any thesis concerning its authorship" (*IR*, 48).

According to Leibniz, the first question of metaphysics is "Why is there something, rather than nothing?" The answer Jonas gives is not only independent of reference to belief in its divine creation but also hostile to any attempt to provide an answer in theological terms that, in his view, must always beg the question: "For the 'why' asked here can obviously not aim at the antecedent cause, which—itself belonging to the things that are—can be looked for only *within* the realm of being and as accounting for parts or states therein, but never, on pain of contradiction as relating to the totality of things or the fact of being as such. This logical state of affairs is not altered by the doctrine of creation, which does provide an answer for the world as a whole in the divine causative act—only to revive the question with this very regress, namely, for the existence of God himself" (*IR*, 47). And this, in the century of Auschwitz and the Gulag, is just what is most difficult and existentially painful to believe. As Vogel puts it, Jonas's position is that "If rational metaphysics proves insufficient on its own, then no appeal to a Creator will satisfy the nihilist. For if life can be shown to be worthwhile without reference to God, then whether God exists is superfluous to ethics. But if life cannot be shown to be worthwhile without reference to God, then appealing to a benevolent Creator will only provide hollow consolation for our experience of life's worthlessness" (*MM*, 20). A metaphysic and a metaphysically grounded ethics that depends on appeal to divine creation is, of its nature, unable to overcome the challenge of nihilism that, from its origins in the study of Gnosis, is the challenge Jonas's philosophy is intended to meet.

Where then do Jonas's theological writings belong in the corpus of his work? The answer lies not in continuity with his metaphysics but in his philosophical anthropology, his account of human existence in terms of the three self-transcending dimensions of tool, image, and tomb, and the speculations they seem not only to provoke but also, logically, to require. Here let us recall what Jonas says of each of these forms of human interaction with the world. Tool, image, and tomb are "basic forms in which man, in uniquely human fashion, answers and transcends what is an unconditional given for man and animal alike. With the tool he surpasses physical necessity through invention; with the image, passive perception through representation and imagination; with the tomb, inescapable death through faith and piety. . . . Physics, Art, and Metaphysics, primevally foreshadowed by tool, image, and tomb, are here named less for their eventual products known by these names, which may or may not emerge in the contingencies of history, than for their indicating original dimensions of man's relation to the world, each with its own horizon of possibility" (*PE*, 252-53). Considered thus, belief in God is not a logical requirement, still less a presupposition, of metaphysics, but a speculative possibility, whose assurance can only be provided by an act of faith. A naturalistic metaphysics is compatible with such a faith, but neither metaphysics nor faith requires the other in order to be entertained.

Indeed, as Jonas's theological interlocutor Bultmann suggests, consistent acceptance of the one would seem, at first glance, to rule out the other; for while metaphysics depends on an account of the world in terms of its immanent causality, belief in any God beyond the impersonal divine watchmaker of eighteenth-century Deism, as required by Bultmann's own Christian faith in the incarnate divinity of Jesus Christ, involves reference to a miraculous, supernatural intervention in the causal chain, and in that there is, as Bultmann says, "no room left for God's acting." Bultmann's own answer, that God's acting must be thought of as "a non-worldly and transcendent one, which does not take place *between* worldly actions but happens *in* them" as something hidden (*PE,* 155), seems to Jonas both rationally unconvincing and philosophically unnecessary, depending, as it does, on "an exaggerated conception of the tightness and rigidity of worldly causality" that Bultmann inherits from Kant (*PE,* 156). Jonas's answer to this is that "It is up to philosophy to *show* that the laws of nature are quite compatible with neutral threshold situations . . . from which as from a divide the further process could take several directions . . . *all* of them conforming to the constancy laws, if greatly differing in degrees of probability" (*PE,* 157).

The metaphysical opportunity, but not the psychological or biographical motivation for Jonas's own faith, is provided by his conviction that such a model of nature "can be constructed with the preservation of everything that science (not scientistic metaphysics) tells us about nature" (*PE,* 157). As for the motivation, that depends on something quite different—Jonas's abiding assurance that despite the evidence of Auschwitz, in which his mother perished among so many million others, even a Jew can continue to believe in a beneficent creator God, albeit one who is apparently less omnipotent than traditional theology would have us suppose.

There is something both intensely moving and intuitively persuasive about the theology that results, provisional and speculative though Jonas admits it to be. It is a theology that achieves expression late in Jonas's career in a number of essays in which, at last, the "luxury of reason" that is religious belief could be indulged. Of these the two most important are the 1984 lecture, "The Concept of God after Auschwitz: A Jewish Voice" (*MM,* 131-43), and the much more extended study, "Matter, Mind, and Creation: Cosmological Evidence and Cosmogonic Speculation" (*MM,* 165-97), which dates from 1988. There is a certain irony, if not an element of poetic justice, in the fact that both these essays were occasioned by Jonas's popularity and the prestige he enjoyed in postwar Germany, in which he was a native triumphantly returned; for the first was delivered as a lecture in acceptance of the Leopold Lucas Prize at the University of Tübingen, and the second composed as a contribution to an international conference, "Mind and Nature," held in Hannover and sponsored by the Stiftung Niedersachsen.

It would be wholly against the antiprovidentialist spirit of Jonas's work to see in this hard-won contingency a reason for supposing that the history of the world is either more rational or more just than we know it to be. The cries of the murdered innocent and the unpunished crimes of the guilty—those dead, those living, and those still to come—testify to the self-deluding vanity of any such belief. At the same time, it is impossible to reflect on Jonas's life and work without observing that while the course of things is something radically other than the upward pointing tale of reason and progress that a Hegel, a Marx, or a Teilhard de Chardin supposed, in which those who perish are only the incidental victims of the implacable but merciless march of emergent meaning, it is, by the same token, something more than "a tale of sound and fury, signifying nothing." And if, at the end, extinction is to be our fate, as it has been for countless species before us, this will not be because we did not have the opportunity to influence its course.

In his introductory essay to *Mortality and Morality,* Lawrence Vogel situates Jonas's theology in the context of contemporary Jewish theology, indelibly marked by the experience of the Holocaust as the defining event of twentieth-century Jewish history (*MM,* 30–35). In view of its biographical impact on Jonas's life and the broader challenge to continuing Jewish faith in a beneficent creator posed by the Nazis' mass murder of European Jewry, it is impossible to ignore this dimension in Jonas's theological writings, and I shall say something about it later in this chapter. It would nevertheless be wrong to see Jonas's theology as exclusively a Jewish thinker's response to the events of the Holocaust. As my reference to the continuity between Jonas's biologically oriented philosophical anthropology and his theological writings is intended to suggest, the relationship between Jonas's identity as a Jew and his vocation as a philosopher is both more complex and more generally significant than such a characterization would seem to indicate. By this I mean that although the particular form taken by his theology, and especially his challenging discussion of what he sees as the intrinsic limits of divine agency in the affairs of the world, is deeply marked by his reflections on the events of his time, there is much more to his theological writings than might be supposed if we were to see them as merely a variant of the sort of post-Holocaust theology in which so many theologians, Christian as well as Jewish, have been engaged, at times obsessively, since the end of the Second World War.

In what follows, I shall not presume to judge how far the theology of Jonas is compatible with the teachings of either Jewish or Christian religious orthodoxy. That is a question for others to decide. What is more important in the present context is to point out the extent to which the perspectives of his theological writings, and their evident centrality in his work, stand in continuity with themes in European thought that have formed part of the intellectual heritage of philosophy long before the events of twentieth-century history and that can be traced back beyond the emergence of either Jewish or Christian religion to the origins of Western philosophy among the reflections of the ancient Greeks.

In his seminal book *God and Philosophy* (1941), Étienne Gilson has charted, with exemplary clarity, both the manner in which the rational reflection on man's nature and position in the cosmos that is metaphysics has always involved an opening upon theological issues and the characteristically different ways in which the relationship between theology and metaphysics was successively conceived in ancient Greek, in medieval Christian, and in modern post-Cartesian philosophy, down to contemporary times. In keeping with my own characterization of Jonas's thought as, at once, an authentically modern philosophy and one of retrieval, I believe that we will only grasp the full significance of his theological writings when we see them not simply as conditioned by the events of his time but as embodying his determination to develop for his contemporaries an equivalently integral understanding of man's being in the world no less inclusive of its intrinsically theological dimension. At the same time, unlike the overtly Christian stance maintained by the neo-Thomist Gilson, Jonas's understanding of the range of metaphysical reasoning and reflection falls short of maintaining that belief in God is either implied or required by the exigencies of metaphysics alone. Indeed one of the most challenging features of his teaching is that, while maintaining that such a belief is compatible with what we know of the structure of existence, he insists that the "luxury of reason" that is theology—and thus the supplementary requirement of faith—is distinct even from an overtly metaphysical understanding of what that existential structure implies if it is to be considered intelligible.

Looked at in the context of contemporary theology, Jonas's position is therefore equidistant from that of those who, like Gilson, maintain that a rational metaphysics of existence implies a commitment to
religious belief, and that of theologians, like Bultmann or, still more
radically, of Karl Barth, who see metaphysics and faith as incommensurate and even intrinsically opposed engagements of mind. Indeed,
if anything, the language of Jonas's theology, with its invocation of
the necessity and desirability of what, in "Immortality and the
Modern Temper," he terms a "tentative myth which I would like to
believe 'true'" (*PL*, 278), recalls nothing else in twentieth-century
thinking. Rather, it recalls the recourse to myth that was, for Aristotle, such a troubling feature in the thought of Plato and his consequent wager of belief, foreshadowing that of Pascal, that such a
myth may nevertheless be not only plausible but true. Where it differs from either Plato's myths or Pascal's wager is in seeking to show
that acceptance of such a theology, and of the possibility of religious
faith it implies, is consistent with an understanding of the nature of
the world informed by the apparently godless discoveries of a naturalistic science that conceives reality in terms of contingent, material processes alone. In "The Concept of God after Auschwitz" and
"Matter, Mind, and Creation," Jonas argues not only that such a theology is internally coherent but also that it can be reconciled both
with the challenge of a secular history devoid of providential consolation and with the best evidence of the contemporary physical
sciences of nature.

Among major philosophers of the twentieth century, only Eric
Voegelin maintains anything like a comparable position, but, in contrast to Jonas, Voegelin's account of the inherent logic of the process
that he calls "meditation" and his exposition of what Plato might
have meant by his notion of a "true myth," while rational and generally persuasive, is both couched in a language redolent of Platonic theology and largely devoid of the systematic reference to the evidence of current natural (as opposed to historical) science that is
such a notable feature of Jonas's in many ways similar undertaking.
This is both a strength and a weakness in Voegelin's philosophy,
which, in comparison with that of Jonas, gains in rhetorical consis-
tency what it loses by seeming to abstract his theologically informed
anthropology from the worldview of contemporary science.

As it happens, this perceived loss is more apparent than real, but though there is nothing in Voegelin's philosophy of history as a "mystery in process of unfolding," as opposed either to those of his nineteenth-century precursors Hegel and Schelling or to his contemporary Heidegger's "history of Being" that is incompatible with the implications of natural science, this crucial point can be all too easily missed by readers attuned to a more overtly secular philosophical idiom than that which Voegelin habitually employs. In an intellectual environment conditioned by the legacy of positivism to be distrustful of all theological reference in what purports to be an empirically based science of man and nature, this at least is a rhetorical disadvantage that Jonas avoids; if the price he pays for this avoidance is reliance on the philosophically familiar language of a metaphysical tradition inherited from Aristotle, which Voegelin, hardly less than Heidegger, regards as both unduly naturalistic and fatally anthropocentric, the price is one worth paying.

Indeed if there is one defining feature of Jonas's philosophy that distinguishes it both from that of Heidegger and from Voegelin, it is his unfashionable but necessary conviction that it is the language of an apparently naturalistic metaphysics that can alone provide philosophy with a means of integrating adequately the apparently discrete spheres of scientific knowledge and theological speculation in an integral and inclusive account of man's being in the world. This is not to say that Jonas is unaware of the innate shortcomings of metaphysics as a discipline to whose inevitably speculative and provisional character both Voegelin and Heidegger, in keeping with the vast mass of contemporary thinkers, can so readily point. Rather his position is that, despite these limitations, the language of metaphysics is the best we have or are likely to get in seeking to articulate as rationally as we may the abiding contours of our ultimately mysterious world.

I am, alas, only too aware of how perversely unfashionable this view must seem. Nor is this at all surprising when so much conspires to make it so. I spoke earlier of the present academic scene as marked by what I called "the entropy of knowledge," characterized by an ever greater division of the realm of learning along disciplinary lines and a consequent breakdown of communication between researchers in different fields. Jonas, I suggested, was an exception to this rule, not only by virtue of the range of his writings, covering, as they do, studies of areas as apparently diverse as the history of ancient religious creeds and the ethical implications of current developments in biological science, but also because of his no less apparent ambition to integrate the lessons he derives from each of the regions to which he is drawn. Nor is this ambition to be dismissed as the sign of an amateurish eclecticism in which the conclusions of one field of inquiry are transposed more or less arbitrarily into the sphere of another. Rather it reflects a single effort, rooted in Jonas's awareness of what he sees as the nihilistic implications of Heidegger's existentialism, to articulate for his time a more rational and ethically responsible philosophical account of man's being in the world. There is indeed a sense in which everything that Jonas wrote is marked by this sustained attempt to escape not the valid insights of Heidegger's reformulation of philosophy along existential lines, but the metaphysically fatalistic and morally fatal conclusions to which his first mentor was eventually and, as it seems, implacably drawn.

George Steiner has spoken of what he calls the ubiquitous "presence of Heidegger" on the current philosophical scene—a presence evidenced not merely by Leo Strauss's culturally acute observation that "the only great thinker in our time is Heidegger," but by the plethora of postmodernist philosophies that share, if little else, an assumption that Heidegger has rendered obsolete all previous attempts, whether by metaphysics, theology, or anthropology, to provide an overall account of man's being and destiny. And this alone should make us attentive to what Jonas has to say. Moreover, Jonas's philosophy is characterized not just by a powerful argument that systematically vindicates, against Heidegger, the legitimacy of metaphysical speculation, but also by being both attentive to the cognitive implications of modern science and couched in an intelligible style agreeably remote from the arcane jargon of Heidegger and his disciples; these traits make it more relevant still. When, in addition, one considers that this philosophy culminates, if not in proof of the existence of God, then at least in a sense of the rational plausibility of religious belief, one can only wonder by what miracle of contemporary perversity it is not better known.

All these features of Jonas's thought are triumphantly exemplified in his late essay "Matter, Mind, and Creation" (*MM*, 165–97), which dates from 1988 and which, despite its relative brevity, can even more than *The Imperative of Responsibility* be considered the ultimate consummation of his life's work. The essay not only contains, as the book does not, an articulation of the explicitly theological dimension of his philosophy; it also situates his understanding of man's being against the background of more than just a philosophy of life—a philosophical biology. It embraces a cosmology that recognizes the universal properties of inert matter—a philosophy of physics.

At several points earlier in this book, I have called attention to the parallels between Jonas's work and the equivalently biologically informed philosophy of Aristotle. Reading "Matter, Mind, and Creation," one is struck by an even more astonishing parallel, between the philosophy of Jonas and the thinking of the pre-Socratic philosophers with whom the adventure of Western thought began. For there is indeed a real sense in which Jonas, writing in the late twentieth century, seems in the range of his thought to resume, not the surmised teaching, but the encyclopedic ambitions of Thales, the first recorded thinker of the West, of whom we know from Aristotle only that he believed, first, that the ultimate physical constituent of the world, from which all else arises and to which it returns, was water, and, second, that "all things are full of gods."

What precisely Thales may have meant by these observations is a matter for continuing scholarly dispute, which need not concern us here. What is more significant in the present context is that, when looked at in terms of our current disciplinary division of labor, his first hypothesis belongs to the realm of physics and his second to theology; and that both apparently formed part of an overall philosophical account of reality that a later, more conceptually differentiated thinker like Aristotle could regard as exemplary for his own. Fortunately in the case of Jonas, we have something more substantial than the two fragmentary utterances that remain to us from the work of Thales. But what is striking about "Matter, Mind, and Creation" is that while neither Jonas's emphatically modern physics nor his monotheist theology is that of Thales, he shares with philosophy's first master a conception of the range of philosophical reflection that encompasses both an account of the elementary constituents of the physical universe and a doctrine of divine presence in the scheme of things. Both seem to Jonas essential components of an existentially complete theory of man's worldly being, and both, in Heidegger, are notable for their absence.

Despite this, I believe that we must look to Heidegger if we are to grasp adequately the impelling force of the argument that guides "Matter, Mind, and Creation"—specifically, to what I have termed Heidegger's reformulation of philosophy along existential lines. It is quite apparent, from the number and quality of Heidegger's one-time students, not only from their personal testimony, moving though that often is, but from the range and originality of the independent work that the best of them produced, that Heidegger was not just the most influential thinker of his generation but perhaps the greatest teacher of philosophy of his or any time. Faced as we are today with a mass of all but unreadable texts, some regrettably from Heidegger's own pen, many more from those who purport, with more or less justification, to be his faithful interpreters and followers, it is all too easy to bemoan the generally nefarious effect of his legacy on both the style and content of much current philosophical writing. But this is to forget the other, ultimately more important, side of the coin—the degree to which the best of his work challenges and indeed requires us to reexamine issues and authors that more conventional scholarship had consigned to the tender but mortifying process of monographic embalmment of which most history of philosophy consists.

If some of us remain convinced that the great monuments of Western philosophy, and many of the lesser ones as well, are something more than the detritus left behind, as certain feminist and multiculturalist writers charge, by a number of overvalued "dead white males," it is an assurance we owe, in part, to the vivifying impact of Heidegger's readings and equally challenging misreadings of these works. Even the most outrageous and far-fetched of his interpretations of the thinkers and thoughts of the philosophical tradition are animated by the generous conviction that their ideas, like his own, were rooted in the innately human need to seek to find some intelligible order in the fragile and ultimately fatal business of mortal existence. Nothing could be more removed from the dry academicism and obsession with linguistic technicalities—logic for its own sake—that marks the practice of the holders of some of our most esteemed university chairs, as it seemed to Heidegger to disfigure the work of the high-minded neo-Kantian thinkers preeminent in the German universities of his youth. Such philosophy is all very well, but what, asked Heidegger of himself and his students, has it to say about the urgent and most personal concerns of our lives—lived, as they are, in a succession of self-made choices resolutely decided, or evaded, against the horizon of ultimate, inescapable death?

With the notorious exception of his brief period as the Nazi rector of Freiburg University and would-be philosophical führer of Hitler's New Order—a ludicrously grandiose and lamentable ambition that such lesser, but more politically astute, figures as Rosenberg, Bäumler, and Krieck were determined that he was never going to achieve—Heidegger never taught his students blindly to accept his answers as commands from on high. Rather, he sought to awaken in them the questions he had made his own, which were those that he disclosed, and believed he had discovered, in the texts he interpreted. More than this, he tried—with remarkable success, to judge by the evidence of the work of such ex-students as Jonas, Hans-Georg Gadamer, and Leo Strauss—to teach them to see these questions anew, not as mere historical curiosities fit for academic inquiry alone but as essential, if enigmatic, dimensions of existence, matters not to be abstractly pondered but concretely lived as part of the adventure of a philosopher's life. This is something that the more reverential exegetes of Heidegger often seem inclined to forget.

Heidegger's best students, and those he seems to have respected the most—and Gadamer is here exemplary in this regard—were not those who parroted his teaching as though it were holy writ, but those who rethought in their own right questions he had implanted in their minds, even when the answers at which they arrived were different from his own. Heidegger was never in any sense a political liberal, but he prided himself on being a liberating educator, whose greatest pedagogic aim was to teach his students where and how to question and rethink the fundamental issues of human thought and existence. In this respect, Jonas was an authentic product of his master's art, and never more so than in the persistence with which he pursued his own very different answer to the question of man's being in the world broached with such profound force and such abiding influence in *Being and Time*.

If this excursus on Heidegger's role as an educator has seemed a digression in the context of a chapter on Jonas's theology, this would be a misunderstanding not just of Jonas's theology but of his whole work, of which it forms an integral part. For that work is animated by a sustained attempt to provide an answer to Heidegger's question concerning Being by way of man's being-there-in-the-world, *Dasein,* that is the theme of his existentialist masterpiece, *Being and Time*. Jonas's answer is at once more comprehensive and more rational than Heidegger's own, not in its characterization of man as such but in its admission of dimensions of the world experience—physical, biological, and theological—that are fatally absent from Heidegger's account.

I do not want here to go into the reasons why Heidegger's account of the "world" of human existence is so abstracted from so many of the objective features of physical being—nature as such—that we normally attribute, rightly, to what we take the world to be. I have said enough in previous chapters, especially on organic being and the philosophy of life, to indicate that Jonas has little time for the kind of existentialist sophistry that empties the so-called world of *Dasein*'s existence of all reference to its basis in organic being and its contextual placement in the supporting world of physical processes. The ethics of responsibility for the integrity of nature developed in *The Imperative of Responsibility* is, after all, rooted in Jonas's conviction that the continuing integrity of man himself depends on the cultivation of respect for the objective properties of nature of which man is an evolutionary product and of which he remains an integral though uniquely self-conscious and powerful component part.

Heidegger, in *Being and Time*, claims to provide what he calls a "fundamental ontology" of *Dasein*. But this, in Jonas's view, is a strangely disembodied ontology, hardly an ontology at all, because it seems to picture the authentic being of *Dasein* in exclusively temporal terms of its projected being-toward-death, without, as Plessner observes, noting that only a living being—a peculiarly self-conscious form of organism—can be said to achieve authentic existence through appropriating awareness of its own mortality. There is something a little mysterious, not to say ontologically obscurantist, in privileging, as Heidegger does, that being's awareness of its own mortality while ignoring its no less self-constitutive awareness of all the other manifold processes that compose its being as a living body and its distinctiveness as one form of life among others.

In Jonas's view as in Plessner's, it is the function of a philosophical anthropology to identify the distinctive form of organic being that is man's. And here let us recall again Max Scheler's classic definition of philosophical anthropology as "a basic science which investigates the *essence* and essential constitution of man, his relationship to the realms of nature (organic, plant and animal life) as well as the source of all things, man's metaphysical origin as well as his physical, cultural and social evolution along with their essential capabilities and realities." Heidegger's characterization of man as *Dasein,* being-there, ignores the fact that he is situated in the world as a particular, essentially distinct type of being, *Sosein,* in a particular objectively structured world, in which he orients himself through the three dimensions of equally distinctive activity that Jonas identifies primevally with the making of tools, images, and tombs.

Each of these is an "artificially mediated way originating from invention and open to further invention," through which man, "in uniquely human fashion," copes with the world in which he finds himself and so, within the limit set by his own mortality, masters his fate as best he may. Plessner has a phrase characterizing the being of man that also essentially encapsulates Jonas's view. Plessner's term is "the mediated immediacy" of man's being in the world, which he distinguishes from the simple immediacy of other forms of animal being. This corresponds to the German distinction, established by the philosophical biologist Jacob von Uexkhull, a seminal figure in the development of the discipline of philosophical anthropology, between the environment, or *Umwelt,* of the animal and the world, or *Welt,* of man. This distinction draws attention to the fact that while the animal inhabits an environment of more or less pleasant sensations to which it is either drawn or repelled in accord with the survival needs of its organic being, man inhabits a world of objects whose more or less measurable properties he estimates in terms of their essential character. This is not to say that man does not also respond to the brute immediacy of the stimuli of sensation, heat and cold, hard and soft, painful or pleasurable, either to which he is drawn or from which he seeks to escape. Rather, the point is that, for man, these stimuli are perceived to emanate from identifiable objects that, by means of conceptual language, he names, and that, by means of practical experiment and theoretical inquiry, science, he objectively identifies in terms of their innate structural properties.

This humanly specific feature of world consciousness explains why language is inherently and necessarily an objectifying medium, through which the human subject forms for himself a picture of the world of objects, which he can subsequently manipulate insofar as he correctly identifies their objectively given properties, and to which he can add, practically, through the use of the tools he constructs for this purpose, and imaginatively, in the form of works of art.

In his essay "Heidegger and Theology" (*PL*, 235–61), Jonas criticizes Heidegger's attribution to Plato of this feature of objectification as an alienating distortion of man's primal awareness of his embeddedness in the flow of being. From this the "illusions" of objectifying metaphysics are said to derive, and these in turn are said to engender an age of global technology, "forgetful of Being," in which the things of the world are evaluated in terms of their use value alone. However, the subject-object relation, enshrined as a distinction or duality in the language of the metaphysical tradition, "is not a lapse but the privilege, burden and duty of man. Not Plato is responsible for it but the human condition, its limits and nobility under the order of creation. For far from being a deviation from Biblical truth, this setting of man over against the sum total of things, his subject-status and the object-status and mutual externality of things themselves, are posited in the very idea of creation and of man's position vis-à-vis nature determined by it: it is the condition of man *meant* in the Bible, imposed by his createdness, to be accepted, acted through—and transcended only in certain encounters with fellow beings and God, i.e., in existential relations of a very special kind. The philosopher's respect for the Biblical tradition rests precisely on the acknowledgement of the role it has played in impressing this ontological scheme with its great and exacting tension upon the Western mind—more so, perhaps, because more unambiguously than even the Greek tradition. The origin of the rift, whether deplored or hailed, is in Moses no less than in Plato. And if you must lay technology at somebody's door, don't forget, over the scapegoat of metaphysics, the Judaeo-Christian tradition" (*PL*, 258–59).

I have cited this argument against Heidegger's denigration of the human propensity to objectify the relationship between man and world at some length for a number of reasons. First, it shows with absolute clarity the relationship that Jonas sees between the biblical doctrine of the divine creation of world and man and the metaphysical recognition of the innate duality between subject and object. Second, it attributes to the awareness of this distinction the uniquely Western development of a practically oriented science and its concomitant achievement in the form of global technology. And third, against Heidegger, it sees this worldview not as symptomatic of a "forgetfulness of Being" but as registering the simple and inalienable truth of the human condition. It is not Plato or Moses who has made it so but the reality of nature that the biblical tradition identifies as the order of divine creation. In this scheme, man occupies a special position not because his being is any more necessary than that of any other life-form but because he alone is aware of the order of the whole, which he may or may not choose to regard as the product of divine creation. Either way, his essential nature and condition is the same, and it is useless to seek in utopian fashion to rebel against it. This is the innate realism shared by the biblical tradition with the worldview of naturalistic metaphysics and against which the tempestuous voices of revolutionary visionaries rail and rebel in vain. It is this latter phenomenon that Eric Voegelin describes as "revolutionary gnosticism" and that he identifies as the spiritual source of the disorder of modern times.

In Jonas's own life, this disorder was manifested most painfully in the phenomenon of National Socialism. Jonas himself left Hitler's Germany in 1933. His parents did not, and his mother perished in Auschwitz, a victim of the Nazis' bloodlust against the Jews. It is impossible to imagine how Jonas's life and thought might have developed without the impact of the Third Reich; although, as I have suggested, he would in all likelihood have pursued a relatively conventional career in the comfortable environment of the German university system, pursuing, as established German professors were able to do, the lines of research to which he was originally drawn. As it happened, things turned out quite differently. The struggle against a murderous regime, in which his life as a Jew was especially at stake, led him not just to five years of soldiering, but to consideration of the intrinsically risky phenomenon of life as such and the conditions under which its continuation could be assured.

This, one may say, was Jonas's response as a philosopher to the events of his time. But there was, beyond this, his response as a theologian, and a specifically Jewish theologian at that. Of course, the two cannot be so neatly separated, for, as we have seen, Jonas sees exploration of the theological dimension of human existence—the question of man's relationship to God—as an integral part of the philosopher's task of giving an account of the contours of man's being. This conviction is not merely a function of his faithfulness to a philosophical tradition in which, until very recently, consideration of the problem and mystery of God's existence, and of his relationship, if any, to the world, has always played a central role. Rather the specific character of his philosophical anthropology, with its characterization of human distinction within the animal realm in terms of the three coeval dimensions of activity exemplified by the tool, the image, and the tomb, sensitized him, with the third, to the humanly constitutive propensity of man to "meditate on life and death, defy appearance and elevate his thought to the invisible" (*PE*, 252).

For the Jew in mid-twentieth-century Europe, the age of Hitler and the extermination camp, the outstanding problem of God was, of course, not merely his invisibility but his apparently total absence at the time of the mass martyrdom of his chosen people, when their need for him was greater, perhaps, than ever before. It is this experience that gives a special poignancy to the title, "Is Faith Still Possible?" (*MM*, 144-64), that Jonas gave to the memorial lecture that he delivered in November 1976 in memory of his friend and colleague, the Christian theologian Rudolf Bultmann, who had died at age ninety-one the previous July.

Just as Jonas's work as a philosopher can be read in one significant sense as an extended dialogue with Heidegger, so his theological writings bear signs of his sympathetic if critical dialogue with Bultmann. "Is Faith Still Possible?" is subtitled "Memories of Rudolf Bultmann and Reflections on the Philosophical Aspects of His Work." And, as this dual designation indicates, this memorial lecture is something more than a personal tribute to a man Jonas regarded with both affection and respect, though it is certainly that as well.

Jonas first encountered Bultmann in 1924 when he entered the older man's Marburg seminar on the New Testament. Already primarily a philosopher and a disciple of Heidegger, whose portrait he drew in a vividly intense sketch in profile that appears reproduced on the sleeve of the English translation of Heidegger's *Fundamental Concepts of Metaphysics* (1995), Jonas was already interested in religion, though, as he says, "according to my origins," this interest had hitherto "been practised in Old Testament and Judaic studies" (*MM,* 145). It was, he adds, Bultmann who "opened the New Testament to me. What I know of it and, as a non-Christian, perhaps understand, somehow stems from him. And with the New Testament, he also opened up to me the historical stage of primitive Christianity, and therewith the theme that was to hold me in thrall for so long" (*MM,* 145). It was in Bultmann's seminar that Jonas presented what he recalls as "an immoderately long seminar" on knowing God in the fourth, Johanine, Gospel, and it was Bultmann's encouragement to pursue this theme that drew him into the study of Gnosis.

Jonas's study of free will in St. Augustine, first presented in Heidegger's seminar, was published in the series of research studies that Bultmann edited, and it was again Bultmann who ensured the publication, in 1934, of Jonas's first volume on Gnosticism. Despite the risk he ran in associating his name with the work of a Jewish author, Bultmann contributed a preface to that work. This, it may be recalled, was at a moment when Jonas's first mentor, Heidegger, was at the height of his enthusiasm for the Nazi cause; during this time, Heidegger, as the new rector of Freiburg University, signed the decree that banned, among others, his own old master, Edmund Husserl, from the use of the university's library and, perhaps more shamefully still, removed Husserl's name from the title page of *Being and Time.* It is small wonder that Jonas, who knew too well what was at stake in all this, even if he could not have suspected the horrors to which it would eventually lead, always held Bultmann in high regard, speaking of "the unwavering purity of his being," and as one of "the untainted few" whom he revisited, in his British officer's uniform, on his return to Germany in 1945.

Jonas has left us with a touching picture of the circumstances in which he took his leave of Bultmann and his family before beginning his exile. "It was in the summer of 1933. . . . We sat around the dinner table with his lovely, so richly emotional wife and their three schoolgirl daughters, and I related what I had just read in the newspaper, but he not yet, namely, that the German Association of the Blind had expelled its Jewish members. My horror carried me into eloquence: In the face of eternal night (so I exclaimed) the most unifying fate there can be among suffering men, this betrayal of a common fate—and I stopped, for my eye fell on Bultmann and I saw that a deathly pallor had spread over his face, and in his eyes was such agony that the words died in my mouth. I knew that in matters of elementary humanity one could simply rely on Bultmann, that words, explanations, arguments, most of all rhetoric, were out of place here, that no insanity of the time could dim the steadiness of his inner light. He himself had not said a word. Ever since, for me this episode has belonged to the image of the inwardly moved but outwardly un-emotional man. (It was certainly not kinship of temperament that bound me so affectionately to the restrained, by appearance almost cool, native of Oldenburg)" (*MM*, 146).

This is not a biography of Jonas. Nevertheless the episode of his leave-taking from Bultmann and his family is worth relating in the context of a discussion of Jonas's theology. For Jonas's account also throws some light on the type of influence that Bultmann's radically demythologizing theology exercised on the development of Jonas's own theological position. No more than Bultmann's cool reserved tem-perament could his radical separation of theology from his strictly Kantian philosophy of immanent worldly causality satisfy Jonas's own very different conception of the relationship between divine presence and worldly order; and while we cannot, in the present context, go into the details of his criticisms of Bultmann's position, it is important to note that just as the nobility and integrity of Bult-mann's personal moral stance, so different from that of Heidegger, provided Jonas with a model against which he could measure his own stance, so the intellectual rigor with which Bultmann devel-oped his existential theology alongside, and yet apart from, his rigorously rational Kantian philosophy of causality provided Jonas with a model before and against which he could develop his own, more integrated account of how an essentially naturalistic meta-physics, respectful of the causally determined order of the natural world, could yet leave space for a theology of divine presence de-spite the apparently radical contradiction between the two.

Jonas's position here is both subtle and persuasive. He begins with the observation of the difference made by the fact that while Bultmann's position is primarily that of a theologian, deeply im-pressed with the self-sufficiency of the modern scientific account of the world in terms of its immanent causality against which the miraculous supernatural possibility of divine intervention cannot be permitted to transgress, his own essentially philosophical starting point sensitizes him to the limits of what our knowledge of causality may seem to imply. "It may," he says, "seem strange that the philosopher should accord more to the possibility of faith, or accord less weight to its modern impediments, than the theologian, so overawed by the authority of science. It is less strange when one considers that the philosopher knows by profession about the *limits* of knowledge, because he constantly bumps up against them, and therefore is perhaps more immune to the pressure of what is carried along with the mighty prestige of science but is itself a faith" (*MM,* 163). Here the crucial insight, referred to earlier, is that our scientific knowledge of the immanent causality of the world order is not a knowledge of a completely determined causal system in which one already achieved causally determined situation must necessarily imply a single determined outcome. "It is up to philosophy to *show* that the laws of nature are quite compatible with neutral threshold situations . . . from which as from a divide the further process could take several directions . . . all of them conforming to the constancy laws, if greatly differing in degrees of probability" (*PE,* 157).

As it happens, philosophy, especially a philosophy as informed as Jonas's is by awareness of the contingencies of the evolutionary history of life, is able to show just this, for the evolutionary history of life on earth, determined as it is by chance mutations of preexistent biological life-forms, each of which has the possibility, but no more, of generating a novel form more capable of surviving in the preexisting environmental context—itself no less subject to chance mutational changes that are more or less conducive to the survival of given species—is just such a story of "threshold situations," from none of which can the necessary future course of events be predicted. Only in retrospect does one situation appear necessarily to derive from that which preexisted it. Most such changes, deriving as they do from the chance mutations of individual organisms, are infinitesimally small. Occasionally, however, as with the impact of the great comet or meteorite that seems to have caused the extinction of the dinosaurs some 65 million years ago, the effect of the previously unpredictable event—this time extraterrestrial—can be enormous.

What has all this to do with the theological possibility of supernatural divine intervention in the causal order of the world? Nothing itself necessary, and yet possibly everything. Nothing in the

sense that the scientifically warranted evidence that the causal order of the world is something other than a single predetermined
causal chain gives us no reason to believe that such a supernatural
divine intervention ever has occurred. But everything when we consider that the fact that the world order is not univocally determined
at least allows for the possibility of such intervention. Whether we
believe that such interventions have in fact happened is a matter of
faith; but contrary to what Bultmann seems to have assumed, there
is nothing in our knowledge of the world that precludes the possibility of faith that such miracles are indeed possible in a causally determined world. At the least, the causally determined worldview of
modern science would seem to allow this acceptance. And if faith in
supernatural intervention in the causal order of the world is possible, how much more so is the weaker position that the order of natural being, and the special divinely intended place of man within it,
expresses a divine intent?

This is the metaphysical possibility that underlies the admittedly
speculative position that Jonas expresses in his theological writings.
This is, in Jonas's phrase, the "tentative myth I would like to believe
true" (PL, 278), or, in Kantian terms, "the luxury of reason" that in
the latter years of relative ease from which his theological essays date
he permits himself to indulge. It stands in continuity with the scientifically informed metaphysics of his naturalistic metaphysics, not
as a logical requirement but rather as a speculative extension of what
has gone before. What he maintains is plausible, but whether the
reader will find it not only plausible but believe it true depends on
an act of faith that Jonas seems prepared to make but cannot compel
his readers to accept. That, for each, depends on an act of faith of his
own, and such acts of faith are, in the modern world, more the exception than the rule—the more so, given the multitude of historical happenings, of which the events of the Holocaust are only one
striking example, that make any such act of faith so difficult to make.
It is a tribute to Jonas's fidelity to his Jewish heritage that he, at least,
is prepared to maintain such a position of faith; but even in his case,
the faith that informs his theology involves sacrificing the doctrine
of divine omnipotence that has traditionally formed part of Jewish
and Christian orthodoxy alike. This is the price he believes he must
pay in order that his belief in the existence of a beneficent divine
creator may be maintained.

The occasion for Jonas's most systematic statement of this theological position, "Matter, Mind, and Creation," occurred when he was sent, in 1987, a document entitled "Outline on the Theme: Cosmos and the Second Main Principle." Jonas's essay, first presented in abbreviated form in May 1988 at a congress held in Hannover called "Mind and Nature," was his response to the thesis of that document. It is, in some ways, the most complex of all of Jonas's many essays, not because it is unclear, but because, in its range, which extends from considerations of physics to a highly personal theological speculation informed by the case of Etty Hillesum, a young Dutch Jewish woman who was sent to the gas chamber at Auschwitz in 1943, it encompasses a lifetime's reflection on the question of man's being in the world that was Jonas's legacy from the teaching of his master Heidegger. Jonas's text is both logical and passionate, and it embodies a synthetic response to this question along lines more cognitively inclusive, more rational, and more ethically sensitive than Heidegger's own. Nothing that I can say in summary of his position can provide a substitute for reading in full what is, by any standard, one of the most remarkable documents of twentieth-century philosophy. Nevertheless, I shall try in what follows to bring out some of the main steps in the argument he develops—an argument that is consistent both with what I understand to be the present state of scientific knowledge and, with the important exception of Jonas's rejection of divine omnipotence over the created order, also with the Judeo-Christian hypothesis that the universe is the creation of a beneficent God in whom we may believe.

As this characterization will indicate, Jonas's essay is an astonishingly ambitious undertaking that has no equivalent in any other writing I know. It is provocative, rational, and wise, but at the same time it leaves one at the end with as many questions as it seems to answer. In this sense, it reflects the enigmatic quality that characterizes the being of man as a creature who, by fate and condition, participates in a process of existence that, despite his best efforts, he never fully understands. Recalling here the terminology of Eric Voegelin, the condition of man's participation in being is that the process in which he participates is a "mystery in process of unfolding" into whose form, structure, and ultimate destiny he may gain certain insights but which, at the limit, extends beyond, or transcends, his powers of knowing. A characteristic feature of Jonas's engagement with this theme is the care he takes to distinguish the point at which knowledge ceases and the task of speculation begins, and his no less characteristic conviction that, provisional though it must be, such speculation is part of the authentic vocation of man.

It is not only the content of Jonas's essay that is interesting but its structural form as well, and it is worth saying something about this in order to convey the full measure of what Jonas is seeking to do in "Matter, Mind, and Creation." In their metaphysics the medieval scholastics, like Aristotle before them, distinguished the order of perception from the order of being. By this they drew attention to the fact that the order in which we perceive the world is not the order in which it comes to be. When we perceive the world, what we perceive is the achieved effect of prior causes. Thus while perception works, as it were, backward, from empirically knowable effects to what must have been their prior causes—material, formal, and final or purposive-teleological—in the actual order of the world's being, the cause must logically precede the effect.

In the metaphysics of Aristotle, the ultimate first cause is posited as being the prime mover, an impersonal causal principle that is itself eternal, unmoving and unmoved. In the Christian, Jewish, and Islamic philosophies of the Middle Ages, the place of the prime mover is taken by the personal being of the creator God. In this way, the conception of the cosmos derived from Aristotle comes, in his nonpagan successors, to be identified with the divinely intended, purposeful creation of the God of the Bible and the Koran. It is this innate purposefulness of all creation that modern science seems most decisively to reject. As we have seen, the Darwinian theory of evolution through natural selection enabled, for the first time, this rejection of purposeful design to be extended from the mechanistic universe of inert matter, as conceived philosophically by Descartes and enshrined in Newtonian mechanics, to the world of living nature in which the appearance of functionally fitting design is otherwise so seemingly exemplified.

As indicated in our chapter on organic being, this is a view of things that Jonas fully accepts; and that is why he found untenable the thesis proposed in the document he was sent, from Germany, in 1987, which seemed to him incompatible with the antiteleological ontology of modern physics. In its quest to establish a hypothesis that would explain the tendency of nature to create from purely physical structures, originating in the so-called Big Bang, structures of increasing organizational complexity—such as the phenomenon of life—"Cosmos and the Second Main Principle" posited that, at its point of origin, "there had also arisen, apart from the total energy of the cosmos, the *information* that would lead to further developments" (*MM*, 165). Jonas recognized in this idea of an immanent "cosmogonic logos"—a primordial in-forming principle—a "first cousin" of the idea of a "cosmogonic eros" first coined by Ludwig Klages.

Jonas would have been familiar with Klages's philosophy of life, which enjoyed a considerable popularity in the Germany of his youth. Nor is it difficult to understand why a revival of such ideas, in the form of the notion of a "cosmogonic logos" operative from the beginning in the order of creation, should exert a certain appeal to those seeking to explain the otherwise mysterious emergence of organic being from previously inert energy and matter. For what the hypothesis seems to do is to remedy the great lacuna of modern science—its apparent inability to explain the great mystery that bisects the realm of chemistry; and, thereby, it seems to explain and bridge the ontological gulf that exists between the properties of inorganic and those of self-regenerating, organic compounds.

The properties of inorganic compounds are ultimately explicable in purely physical terms. They may recombine with others, forming essentially different compounds, and, depending on their degree of stability, are, at concomitantly variable rates, subject to the ultimately entropic pressures of decay that operate, in consequence of the Newtonian laws of thermodynamics, as well on the physical elements of which they are wholly composed. Their reactions are therefore susceptible to explanation exclusively in terms of chemical reactions, themselves ultimately explicable in terms of the physics of the elements of which they are made up. Thus, in essence, explanation of their behavior pertains, in the last resort without remainder, to the domain of physics.

Organic compounds, by contrast, are living substances—the stuff of life. As such, they manifest properties of self-regeneration, in which the continuing identity of the compound is assured by the ingestion of nonidentical material not originally its own. This is the process of metabolism that is, as Jonas shows, the universal, specific difference of the manifold phenomena of life. Furthermore, they may mutate and so form novel organic forms. This characteristic is exemplified alike in the formation of cancerous cells and, at a higher level, in the emergence of new, unprecedented life-forms; some of which may, depending on their fitness for survival in a given environment, survive and even displace the originals from which, through mutation, they derive. It is this that the Darwinian hypothesis of evolution through natural selection explains.

What neither Newtonian physics nor Darwinian evolutionary biology of itself explicates is the transition from inorganic to organic compounds. Hence the appeal of a second primordial formative principle, immanent in the order of creation, such as the idea of a "cosmogonic logos." It is this superficially attractive hypothesis to which Jonas seeks to respond and that he sums up as follows: "From the 'chaotic explosion' this information would lead, at first, beyond the immaterial forms of energy and primordial particles progressively differentiated from them to protons, to hydrogen atoms, and from these to the formation of further ordered systems, such as the periodic table of elements, inorganic compounds, and the beautiful world of crystals. Eventually this information would yield unified *cycles:* in the universe the astronomical cycles, and here on Earth the atmospheric and life cycles, in particular" (*MM*, 165–66).

Put briefly, the problem with this idea is that, though logically it would seem to explain what is otherwise inexplicable, there is, ontologically speaking, nothing in the properties of the inert, energized matter that emerges from the Big Bang to suggest that such a second informative principle actually exists. It is a plausible myth that retains its purely logical plausibility only so long as we ignore the paucity of evidence for its actual, ontological existence. However, more than this: "The concept of 'information,' i.e., of an already present 'logos,' breaks down from the genetic point of view, but also from the standpoint of logic. In whatever manner a permanent articulation might come about in the individual case, it can only repeat itself, maintain its level, and extend its place in the world. It cannot explain the step beyond itself; for that we have need of a transcending factor that is joined to it and leads to something new" (*MM*, 167). "What," Jonas asks, "could that be? I am inclined to answer that the new comes about more trivially and anarchically, on the one hand, and more mysteriously, on the other, than is suggested by the concept of information or logos, a concept so reasonable in itself, postulated by working back from the result, and ultimately deterministic. The 'trivially and anarchically' apply to the physical side, the 'mysteriously' to the mental side" (*MM*, 167–68).

It is, I suggest, not hard to see where Jonas's argument is leading—on the one hand to recognition of the need to accept, in relation to inert matter, the implications of modern physics, and, relative to the realm of life, the principle of evolution through natural selection alone, and, on the other, regarding the emergence of the mental and spiritual within the world we actually experience, to the superior plausibility of transcendent, perhaps divine, creation as preferable to explanation of such phenomena in terms of an immanent informative, cosmogonically primordial "logos" for whose existence we have no evidence and that, even if it did exist, could not logically explain the existence of the qualitatively novel phenomena of subjectivity.

Moreover, there is a further point, not about the direction of Jonas's argument, but about its structural form; and this relates us back to our passing remarks about the Aristotelian and scholastic distinction between the order of being and the order of perception. In beginning, as he does in "Matter, Mind, and Creation," with an account of the properties of inorganic energized matter, the realm of physics, Jonas emphatically endeavors to construct his ontology and, through that, ultimately his theology not, as in more conventional Heideggerian forms of existentialism, along the lines of the order of perception, in which the structure of "world" is deduced from what is most immediately to hand, *vorhanden,* in the being of *Dasein,* but in accord with what modern science understands to be the order of being. On this he is quite clear: "The sequence of the title—matter, mind and creation—should," he says, "indicate the course of the study. It begins with the quantitatively overwhelming aspect of the universe, its *material content* extended in space and time, as natural science describes it. . . . It proceeds to the aspect which announces itself only in the small living part of the natural world . . . , and advances to that which again stands out from the material world, but is still bound to it: the mystery of *mind,* as we know it only in our own self-experience. . . . At this point our investigation raises the question of the creative ground of these stages, i.e., the question of God" (*MM,* 166).

This represents a fundamental reversal, authentically ontological in its concern with the objective properties of being, of the dynamic not just of Heidegger's "fundamental ontology" of *Dasein* but, more radically, of the whole thrust of modern, postmedieval philosophy, which, since Descartes and his dictum "I think, therefore I am," has tended to start with the evidence of subjectivity and deduce therefrom the character and existence of the world. At the same time, in positing the material being of the world, rather than the existence of God as its creative cause, as the primary datum of ontology, Jonas vindicates the primacy of the order of being in a distinctively modern way. Once again, we can recognize the fruitful way in which an element of retrieval—in this case of the priority of the order of being over that of perception—is integrated in a specifically modern, scientifically informed, philosophical account of man's being in the world.

In "Life, Death, and the Body in the Theory of Being," the first essay in *The Phenomenon of Life* (*PL*, 7-26), Jonas draws our attention to how counterintuitive this modern worldview really is, pointing out that "When man first began to interpret the nature of things . . . life was to him everywhere, and being the same as being alive. . . . Bare matter, that is, truly inanimate, 'dead' matter, was yet to be discovered—as indeed its concept, so familiar to us, is anything but obvious. That the world is really alive is really the most natural view, and largely supported by prima-facie evidence. On the terrestrial scene, in which experience is reared and contained, life abounds and occupies the whole foreground exposed to man's immediate view. The proportion of manifestly lifeless matter encountered in this primordial field is small, since most of what we know to be inanimate is so intimately intertwined with the dynamics of life that it seems to share its nature. Earth, wind, and water—begetting, teeming, nurturing, destroying—are anything but models of 'mere matter.' Thus primitive panpsychism, in addition to answering powerful needs of the soul, was justified by rules of inference and verification within the available range of experience, continually confirmed as it was by the actual preponderance of life in the horizon of its earthly home" (*PL*, 7).

Among ancient philosophies, perhaps only Epicureanism, exemplified most systematically in the *De Rerum Natura* of Lucretius, shows any real awareness that life may be no more than a statistically insignificant proportion of that of which the universe is composed—an adventitious and chance adventure set against and within what Nicolai Hartmann memorably calls "the merciless structure of eternity." Even the apparent naturalism of the Stoics, otherwise so poignantly aware of the need to resign oneself disinterestedly before the massively potent order of extra human being, is informed by the belief that this order embodies the providential intention of an ultimately wise world soul. And thus it is hardly surprising that it was to the Stoics, and not the Epicureans, that the early Christian fathers turned in the face of their need to equip themselves philosophically in the intellectually sophisticated world of late antiquity. For Stoicism provided, as Epicureanism did not, a concept of the world as embodying a logos that, as the opening words of St. John's Gospel indicate, could be identified readily enough with the world-creating act of the biblical God. I emphasize again that it is this innate trust in the providentialism of Being that, especially since the Darwinian revolution, the worldview of modern science seems most systematically to disown. The astonishingly bold quality of Jonas's theology, marked as it is by the painful absence of any vestigial evidence of providence in the events of the Holocaust, is a function of his determination, speculatively and tentatively, to redeem the possibility of faith from the wreckage of the providentialist dream of our ancestral Jewish and Christian creeds.

On the intervening links between Jonas's account of the physical structure of the universe and his theological speculation I shall, necessarily, be brief. Such brevity is justifiable because, as he points out, much of what he says summarizes observations that he has previously made in his philosophy of life and his anthropology, and of these we have already spoken in previous chapters. We may say that the distinctiveness of the argument of "Matter, Mind, and Creation" resides on the fact that it transcends, as it were, these observations at both ends—on the one hand, setting the phenomenon of life against the background of its emergence from the broader realm of inert material nature, and, on the other, extending his account of the particular form of life that is man's to the theological question of the relationship of man to God, which is what particularly concerns us here.

All that need be said of the intervening steps of his argument are a few relatively brief remarks. The first is his observation that no such hypothesis as the notion of a cosmogonic logos is required in order to explain why, within the physical universe, organized structures are able to emerge and endure. Here his argument is simple, and, though apparently tautologous, quite sufficient to explain the generation of order from the apparently aimless disorder of the primordial Big Bang that modern physics postulates as the initial cosmic event. "The foundation of all order in nature, of any nature at all," he observes, "lies in the laws of conservation. But these have come to govern because it is only self-conserving reality that conserves itself" (*MM,* 168). In other words, given the initial cosmic event, only those results that are able to endure will, in fact, do so. "Here we have the most primordial and fundamental instance of 'the survival of the fittest.' Order is more successful than disorder. That which has no laws and regularities, and obeys no laws of conservation, could have existed in some arbitrary multiplicity. But as something evanescent it disappears sooner or later and is outlasted by that which has such regularity; what follows laws constitutes nearly all that remains" (*MM,* 168). This is quite sufficient to explain the progressive emergence and endurance of the ordered phenomena of inert nature, particles, atoms, and chemical compounds, and the larger bodies and systems of bodies—planetary systems, for instance—that they compose. Such phenomena are not eternal but merely very long lasting. And the lasting structure that they compose is the physical universe as we know it to be. That such a universe should exist requires the postulation of no teleological principle: simply the endurance of chance-generated order beyond creative disorder.

What, then, of life? Here Jonas distinguishes between the question of life's emergence as such and the explanation he gives for its qualitative distinction in its possession of inwardness or subjectivity. It is the latter that really interests him, and I do not think that his explanation of the former is, any more than any other I know, entirely satisfactory. Briefly what he says is that the time allowed for development of life on Earth, and perhaps elsewhere on the cosmos—though that we do not know—is sufficient for its emergence by pure chance as a result of the residual disorder that permits the emergence of compounds possessing new structural factors that generate the novel properties of life. This, I suggest, may well reflect all we can presently say of the beginnings of life, though there are organic chemists who believe that they can give a more satisfactory account of how this might have occurred and who, in laboratory conditions, claim they can reproduce the primordial generation of self-regenerating organic forms. So far as I know, Jonas says nothing about such efforts beyond warning, on essentially ethical grounds in his essay on "Biological Engineering" (*PE*, 141-67), against the dangers of "playing God" in this way.

We may sympathize with his misgivings about such experiments without accepting, as he seems to do, that Darwinian theory alone already sufficiently explains not only how and why life develops as it does, but also how it first emerges—an answer that to me seems insufficient to explain the qualitative novelty of organic being as such. Nevertheless, for what it is worth, here is what he says. "There was" in the preexisting physical universe "always enough 'disorder' to occasion the formation of new characteristics (structural factors) by accidental, random events, and the momentary successes were subject to the process of selection with its criterion of survival by sheer numbers. *This* is the required 'transcending factor' that leads to the new and then to the higher, and it does so without pre-information, without logos, without planning, even without striving, but only by means of the susceptibility of a given order, already coded for 'information' to a surrounding disorder that forces itself upon it as additional information" (*MM*, 169).

The note appended to this passage refers us to the fact that "with the appearance of self-replicating DNA sequences, the chemical preparation for life has been concluded, and that henceforth 'information science' will itself be the principle for the development of life" (*MM*, 210). That is true enough, except that it does nothing to explain how, primordially, DNA sequences were themselves generated. It seems this is left attributable to the statistically improbable though still admittedly possible chance that such peculiar compounds should, in fact, have appeared. This may indeed be the case, but it is not, of itself, an explanation and is certainly not a Darwinian one. It is, at best, a statistical possibility inherent in the opportunities afforded to chance developments of ordered structures afforded by the considerable, but still not infinite, temporal endurance of a universe subject, ultimately, to "heat death" in consequence of the operation of the second law of thermodynamics. This is important in the overall context of Jonas's argument, which seems, in relation to the mystery of the emergence of life, to preclude from the possibility of purposive, perhaps divine, teleological causality that, at the next stage, he introduces in order to explain that property of living being which he terms "the riddle of subjectivity." This is not a weakness in Jonas's theory, but nevertheless it is a puzzle.

I do not myself see why, though prepared to introduce this speculative possibility as explaining a characteristic defining feature of life, subjectivity, Jonas denies it to the earlier problem of the primordial emergence of life, whose explanation he instead attributes to Darwin, whose theory, dealing as it does with the dynamics of life, *once it already exists,* provides no such explanatory key. The "riddle of subjectivity"—if riddle it be—is only a property of the no less enigmatic riddle of life. The attribution of an enigmatic quality, resistant to naturalistic explanation, to the former but not to the latter seems to me arbitrary and unexplained, and the claim that Darwin can explain the origins of life, but not its subjective property of apparent purposiveness, seems to me plainly wrong. If anything, the reverse would seem to be true, for while the appearance of purposive design, culminating in the possession of subjective purposes of its own by at least one form of uniquely successful organic being, man, is at least susceptible to explanation in terms of the Darwinian principle of natural selection, the primordial emergence of life is not. For that there may indeed be a naturalistic explanation, as yet undiscovered, but it is not one that Darwin provides.

This objection is strengthened by the observation that the creation of novel life-forms, by human biological engineering, is itself explicable in terms of the fact that the efficient agent concerned, man, is himself an inherently purposive being, capable of and willing to exercise design. By analogy, the primordial creation of life would seem prima facie to presuppose the preexistence of an equivalently purposeful being with creative intent, whom theologians call God. The alternative explanation, of life's first emergence as the result of chance alone, is as likely as the emergence of new forms of life in a laboratory as a result of the random mixing of chemicals.

Jonas may be right to reject the notion that such a process can be explained in terms of the primordially present cosmogonic logos. But his reasons for doing so seem to have as much to do with his theological concern to allow room for the operation of a transcendent, divine creative purpose as with the fact that the inert physical universe, the realm of energized matter, alone gives us no evidence to suppose that such an immanent "second principle" actually exists. But, if this is so, then it is hard to say how and why life itself emerges in the history of the world's being beyond the occurrence of a statistically remote possibility. Certainly, Darwin gives no reasons that might explain it. The alternative possibilities are either divine intent or another, cosmically immanent principle or event that still awaits discovery and identification. Both, in principle, are possible, and the oddity of Jonas's position is that accepting neither, he attributes instead a sufficient explanation to Darwin who, so far as I can see, provides no such thing. Nonetheless, the weaker attribution in Jonas's account, the attribution of the emergence of life to the play of chance over time, has at least the merit that, if unlikely, it is not, like the appeal to natural selection—the governing principle of already existing life—simply erroneous.

I shall labor this point no longer. It is an oddity in Jonas's theory, perhaps attributable to his laudable wish to do justice to Darwin's achievement in the face of the scientifically unacceptable objections of some, at least, of his fellow theologians of a more integrally "creationist" stripe. This is perhaps understandable but it does no good to the reputation of Darwinism to attribute to it an explanation at which it neither aims and which it is, by virtue of its confinement to the sphere of existing life, in logical principle and ontological ambition alike, incapable of providing. No more is it conducive to the good of theology, which, if it can be permitted a possible say in explaining the purposive properties of subjectivity, can hardly be denied an equivalent speculative say in explanations of the origin of life. All that need be said is that Jonas is perhaps uncharacteristically inconsistent in allowing divine purpose a possible role in the former but not the latter. And that is a small failing in comparison with his overall achievement in speculative theology. This position, though it might by his own admission be heretical by the ancestral standards of Jewish and Christian orthodoxy, has the merit of saving the possibility of belief in divine creation and in divine beneficence despite the apparent evidence of the terrible century in which Jonas, by force of his own decision to leave Germany, survived and from which we have only now emerged to face the unforeseen challenges of times to come.

Religion teaches us, and moral sensibility requires, that we owe a duty of piety and remembrance to those who have died as martyrs to their faith. But it is not piety, or not piety alone, that leads Jonas to invoke in his theology the memory of Etty Hillesum: a young Dutch Jewish woman, scarcely more than a girl, who, like the better-known Anne Frank, died as a victim of the Nazi persecution of the Jews, and who, again like the rather younger Anne, left behind a journal in which the last events and thoughts of her brief existence are recalled vividly for those who survived. Indeed, given the racial motivation of the Nazi cause, and the indiscriminate way in which murder was visited upon believing and unbelieving Jews alike, and even upon those like Edith Stein, now beatified by the Catholic Church, who had abandoned the faith of their fathers, the very notion of religious martyrdom applied to the case of the Holocaust may be somewhat misguided. For what happened we need another word, and this requirement the tragically apt neologism *genocide*—the murder of a race—has come, historically, to provide as the awful linguistic and juridical legacy of all-too-recent and horribly imitable events.

It says nothing against the poignant domesticity of Anne Frank's diary to remark that, unsurprisingly, the journals of the older Etty Hillesum are informed by a theologically sophisticated reflection on the events in which she was the unwilling but ultimately understanding victim. The evidence of the common humanity of Anne Frank and Etty Hillesum is apparent from the concerns of their respective journals, but no one could either expect, still less require, a girl as young as Anne to rise, beyond describing the routine of domestic life in conditions of the unusual stress brought on by ultimately unsuccessful concealment, to reflection upon the theological implications of the terror of the times as Etty Hillesum was able to do.

As mentioned before, Jonas's mother, like Etty Hillesum, died in Auschwitz—a name that has itself become emblematic only, perhaps, because it was the extermination camp to which the Jews of Central and Western Europe were transported. Unlike the victims from the east who perished at Treblinka, Sobibor, and Belzec, and in the mass shootings of Ukraine, Belorussia, and the Baltic States, the dead of Auschwitz have left relatives, associates, and descendants able and willing to memorialize their lives and the place of their slaughter. As Michael Novick's recent book, *The Holocaust in American Memory,* usefully recalls, the Holocaust has been the occasion for much dubious theology, but, beyond this, it has also been an event that more than any other has required of Christian as well as Jewish theologians a fundamental rethinking of the relations of God and man.

Jonas contributes to this rethinking, but, as I hope I have indicated in my account of his theology thus far, he also does a great deal more than that in contributing to the theological project as a whole. Reflection on the Holocaust—not exactly on its meaning, for in one essential sense it has no intrinsic theological meaning, but on its referential significance in throwing light on the diverging mysteries of the beings of God and man—is, as it were, the jagged edge of his theology. It is the part that existentially pains but, most emphatically, not at all the whole. For if there were no more than the Holocaust to engage the attention of the Jewish theologian, then every rational Jew would understandably be, like Karl Marx and Arthur Koestler, a dogmatic atheist or, perhaps, a latter-day Gnostic enemy of the world's Creator as principle of evil alone.

There is, in Judaism, unlike in Roman Catholicism, no ultimate, authoritative body—no Pope and no General Council of the Church—to lay down the dogmatically necessary articles of religious faith. There is not even a strict equivalent to the Nicene Creed, shared by the various denominations of Christians across their otherwise divergent bodies of practice and belief, beyond the simple declaration of faith in the unity of God in which the religious identity of Judaism essentially consists. This, and perhaps this alone, is the single required article of Jewish belief; as opposed to the multitude of rituals and domestic practices that the observant orthodox Jew is enjoined faithfully to keep. What there is, instead, is a body of more or less authoritative, traditional teachings formulated over centuries by often mutually disputatious rabbis and sages and recorded in the Mishnah and the Talmud. The nearest equivalent in Judaism to such a creed as Christianity possesses is contained in the Thirteen Articles of Faith formulated in the Middle Ages by Moses Maimonides, and, as Jonas notes in "The Concept of God after Auschwitz," it is chanted solemnly in the services of the synagogue (*MM*, 141). This means that it is rather more difficult to be a heretical Jew than a heretical Christian—though the great seventeenth-century Dutch Jewish philosopher, Benedict, or Baruch, Spinoza managed to get himself so declared.

Fortunately, there was in twentieth-century New York no equivalent body to the rabbinical council of seventeenth-century Amsterdam against whom, by his teachings, Jonas might offend. For, judged by the Thirteen Articles of Faith, his theology falls well short of the requirements of orthodoxy. And it is, in large part though not exclusively, his attempt to think through the theological implications of the Holocaust that leads to his considered deviations from certain items of orthodox Jewish belief as enshrined, if not in dogma, then in reverently held tradition.

By formation and inclination, Jonas is primarily a philosopher rather than a theologian, and an existential philosopher educated in the school of Heidegger at that. This means that his primary aim was always to articulate the truth of being, rather than to expound the logic of a particular religious faith. His theology is an extension of his philosophy, and when the implications of his understanding of being conflict with the articles of received faith, it is the demands of hermeneutic insight that carry the greater weight. His position is not unlike that of Paul Ricoeur, a philosopher who is also a believing Christian, who, writing of the relationship between, on the one hand, his philosophy and his politics and, on the other, his regard for the message of the Gospels, observes that one cannot deduce a politics and a philosophy from the Gospel but must rather attend to its message in pursuing the autonomous path of reason that is his vocation as a philosopher. What holds for Ricoeur's attitude to the Gospel holds also for Jonas's attitude toward the Torah and Maimonides' Thirteen Articles of Faith. They may be appropriated critically in the light of reason, but they cannot be allowed to dictate what otherwise he holds to be true.

And there is one more point to make in this context. I spoke of Jonas's theology as being guided and directed in large part, but not exclusively, by his attempt to think through the theological implications of the Holocaust. The qualification indicated by the phrase "not exclusively" refers to the fact that his appropriation of the religion to which he tries to remain faithful is qualified not only by the events of the Nazi onslaught on Jewish existence but also by his understanding of what he takes to be the implications of the modern scientific understanding of man and world. For an existential philosopher, whose questions are determined by the biographically and historically determined pressures of his time, these two elements—response to the Holocaust and rational appropriation of scientific understanding, both of which are equally reflective—cannot be neatly separated. For, as we have seen, Jonas's turn to the philosophy of life, of which his metaphysics and his theology are a logical outgrowth, is itself a function of his felt need to respond to events in which his own life as a Jew was especially threatened. This means that while the core of his Judaism—his confession of the unity of God—remains intact, the Thirteen Articles of Faith enunciated by Maimonides cannot be accepted in full. Some of their propositions must, in Jonas's view, be abandoned in order that their essential core may be retained, even at the cost of the potential charge of heresy.

In "The Concept of God after Auschwitz," he makes explicit what this sacrifice of faith for the sake of reason involves: "For reasons decisively prompted by contemporary experience, I entertain the idea of God who for a time—the time of the ongoing world process—has divested himself of any power to interfere with the physical course of things; and who responds to the impact on his being by worldly events, not 'with a mighty hand and outstretched arm,' as we Jews on every Passover recite in remembering the exodus from Egypt, but with the mutely insistent appeal of his unfulfilled goal" (*MM*, 141).

Jonas's theology responds to the ancient dilemma of the Jewish experience of maintaining belief in a God who begins, promisingly enough, with the assurance of a covenant with his people, the promise of a land that he will deliver, by conquest, into their hands, and the prophecy of his continuing fidelity to their survival in their hour of need. In Jewish history, beset as it is with the experience of temporary triumphs but repeated defeats, only the first of these assurances is in any way religiously secure. The covenant remains, but it is mysteriously emptied of much of its apparent promise. The land is conquered but is subsequently lost, only to be regained after some two thousand years of exile and persecution. And yet, for Maimonides and the voices of orthodoxy, the integrity of belief is maintained in the Thirteen Articles of Faith.

For Jonas, in the aftermath of God's apparent abandonment of his people in the Holocaust, the dilemma of faith is acute, and so the Thirteen Articles are, as it were, pared down to the core of what, in the light of history, can be credibly maintained. "Do not speak to me of the cunning of history," he writes, referring to Hegel's assurance

that every apparent visitation of evil upon the just can be, if not con-
jured away, at least transcended and redeemed by the ultimate historical triumph of what is rational and good. The theologies of the
Holocaust that claim to find in the agony of suffering some covert
religious purpose are, in Jonas's Jewish religious vision, both blasphe-
mous and delusory. And here Jonas is, I think, true to the religious
heritage of Judaism, which, unlike Christianity, has traditionally
little patience with the doctrine of redemptive suffering. History,
Jonas maintains, and the history of suffering and death in particular, is not so easily recast in providential mold. What, then, remains
of the Jewish faith that provides for Hegel, as for every credulous
believer in the ultimate providential triumph of redemptive progress,
the exemplary, first form of their ultimately optimistic faith in redemptive progress? What, too, of Maimonides' Thirteen Articles of
Faith?

Not, to be sure, the "mighty hand and outstretched arm" that
once parted the Red Sea for the passage of the Israelites from Egypt
and toppled the walls of mighty Jericho. No such hand opened the
walls of the Warsaw Ghetto or shattered the railway lines that bore
its survivors to their deaths in the gas chambers. Nor even was the
sign of divine intervention much in evidence in the struggle for
Israel's existence, in which Jonas subsequently participated, on
worldly terms, not as a seer, but as a soldier bearing the arms of war.
And as belief in the efficacy of "the mighty hand" falls away, so do
"the assertions about God's ruling the universe, his rewarding the
good and punishing the wicked," and even "the coming of the Mes-
siah." What remains, however, is "his call to the souls, his inspira-
tion of the prophets and the Torah, thus also . . . the idea of election:
for only in the physical realm does the impotence of God refer. Most
of all the *Oneness* of God remains and with it the 'Hear O Israel!' No
Manichaean dualism is enlisted to explain evil; from the hearts of
men alone does it arise and gain power in the world. The mere permitting, indeed, of freedom involved a renouncing of sole divine
power henceforth. And our discussion of power as such has already
led us to deny divine omnipotence anyway" (*MM*, 141).

Here, in essence, is Jonas's theology of creation, as an originally
divine act by which God sets the world in being and grants to man
the capacity freely to serve or frustrate his beneficent purpose. This
is Jonas's gloss on the biblical idea that man is created in the image

of God, an image whose essence is possession of the shadow of the freedom that once, primordially, called into being the world from the void that was before. The speculation at the core of Jonas's theology is that in so calling the world into being, God puts at risk not his own existence but the fulfillment of his purpose in granting to creation a portion of the autonomy that is originally his own. This places a heavy responsibility on man as the being in whom this autonomy is henceforth most fully vested, with all the risks that this entails. I shall end this chapter with the words from Etty Hillesum's diary that Jonas cites, and on whose wisdom of acceptance he observes only that they seem to confirm the philosopher's continuing duty to speculate, in continuity with man's primordial propensity to "reflect about life and death, defy appearances, and raise his thinking to the realm of the invisible" (*MM,* 85). Such a philosophy, and such a theology, will not satisfy those who, impatient with the mystery of being, seek to confine the realm of thought to what can be verified and assured, and the scope of faith to the easy comfort of cozy dogma. This, though, is the measure of their existential truth, and more we cannot say.

These, then are Etty Hillesum's words, her own unfitting end but perhaps the only fitting conclusion to the theological speculations that have gone before: "I will go to any place on this earth where God sends me, and I am ready in every situation and until I die to bear witness . . . that it is not God's fault that everything has turned out this way, but our fault. . . . And if God does not continue to help me, then I must help God. . . . I will help you, O God, that you do not forsake me, but right from the start I can vouch for nothing. Only this one thing becomes more and more clear to me: that you cannot help us, but that we must help you, and in so doing we ultimately help ourselves. That is the only thing that matters: to save in us, O God, a piece of yourself. Yes, my God, even you in these circumstances seem powerless to change very much. . . . I demand no account from you; you will later call us to account. And with almost every heartbeat it becomes clearer to me that you cannot help us, but that we must help you and defend up to the last your dwelling within us" (*MM,* 192).

7 Philosophy and the Future

In May 1992, Hans Jonas delivered in Munich his lecture "Philosophy at the End of the Century: Retrospect and Prospect." A slightly amended English translation appeared posthumously in the winter 1994 issue of *Social Research,* the journal of the New School for Social Research, at which Jonas had taught as Alvin Johnson Professor of Philosophy from 1954 until his death in 1993. This lecture was subsequently published as a prologue to his collection of essays *Mortality and Morality* (*MM,* 41–55). The publication was a fitting prelude to what remains the best overall selection of the philosopher's writings; in it he provides an overview of his life's work, an account of the intellectual environment in which he had been formed, and, characteristically, an estimation of the future prospects of philosophy as an activity of which mankind would have as much need as ever before.

Cicero began his famous treatise *The Nature of the Gods* by observing, "There are many issues in philosophy which to this day have by no means been adequately resolved." Speaking some two thousand years later, Jonas might well have begun his address by repeating the same notoriously apt understatement, which remains as true today as when first made by the great Roman orator and thinker. Instead, Jonas began by noting some of the intrinsic reasons why this apparently disconcerting fact might be so. Philosophy, he noted, in contrast to the various natural sciences, has neither a specific subject matter nor a single established method of its own. This may be seen as either its weakness or its strength, depending upon what we may reasonably expect from a discipline that seeks to master, not this or that province of reality, but its whole.

Inevitably then, a survey of philosophy's contemporary state and further outlook, such as Jonas was invited to give, would reflect its author's personal experience and perspective, and for this Jonas makes no apology. What he offered was not an index of the present state of accepted knowledge in a defined field but "more a contribution to the never ending discussion of philosophy . . . a confession, in the last analysis, of a personal nature . . . historically incomplete," from which certain important currents of contemporary thinking, notably Anglo-American analytical philosophy, were consciously excluded (*MM*, 42). In this, he reflected not just the accidents of his biography but also the philosophical principle of the existential and phenomenological stance in which he had been educated and to which he had remained true throughout his long career.

As earlier chapters have indicated, Jonas's philosophy is hardly typical of what is commonly understood by either existentialism or phenomenology. Jonas may have been educated, as he puts it, "in the school of such teachers as Husserl, Heidegger and Bultmann" (*PE*, xi), but his thought ventures into fields far from their own and, in particular, pursues forms of metaphysical speculation that each of his acknowledged masters would have regarded, if for differing reasons, as intellectually illegitimate. If, nonetheless, I speak of Jonas's ultimate fidelity to the teachers of his youth, it is because, despite his apparent deviations, his work is marked throughout by a Husserlian determination to remain true to a descriptive analysis of the phenomena—the intentional objects—of consciousness, and by a motivational structure anchored, as Heidegger had taught him authentic philosophy must be, in the existential pressures of his all too mortal being.

There are today many purported scholars of Husserlian and Heideggerian thought, faithful in their way, who follow carefully enough the arguments of these masters but who, in doing so, repeat the verbal forms of their models while losing sight of their referential content—the horizon of human experience itself. The result is a plethora of works—scholastic in the worst sense of that much abused term—that seem, as much as the disembodied technicalities of the products of the analytical school, to remove philosophy from anything approaching either the disciplines of science or the concerns of everyday life, and so render it publicly irrelevant. Husserl's motto, "Back to the things themselves," has a strangely ironic postecho in a context in which the works of so many so-called phenomenologists seem to refer back and forth only to the abstractly technical, literary works of each other. And as for Heidegger, the less said about some of his disciples the better, beyond remarking on their apparent unconcern with the Western tradition of metaphysics and its question of Being from which he could free himself only because he knew it so well.

Compared with these, the work of Jonas evinces a breath of philosophical fresh air, an evident concern with the concrete questions of life, and a taste of stylistic and intellectual literacy unusual in the crabbed and temporally parochial passages of so much current academic literature. Writing out of the experience of his life, his thought, especially on the practical, ethical problems posed by the precipitous advances of modern technology and science, reaches beyond his own times and into a future of which he knew only that he should care that man should endure.

It is this mutually implicatory moral and metaphysical orientation—moral or ethical in its motivation, metaphysical or ontological in its cognitive scope—that is highlighted by the title of Jonas's 1985 essay "Toward an Ontological Grounding of an Ethics for the Future" (MM, 99–112), which summarizes much of the argument of *The Imperative of Responsibility*. The argument here is that man's primary aim must be his own survival as a moral being and that this survival depends upon the care he takes to conserve the integrity of the nature on which his own depends—a nature now subject, as never before, to potentially fatal subversion as a result of the extension, through technology, of human agency into levels of being, including his own genetic structure and the innate capacity of nature to regenerate itself, previously resistant or impervious to human intervention. There is in this an implicit politics—a politics of human survival—that extends, with uncomfortable implications, Jonas's ethical considerations in a way somewhat analogous to the way his theological speculations extend the insights of his anthropology.

I shall end this brief account of Jonas's philosophy with some remarks on what this politics seems to imply, for the political dimension of his ideas, while less developed than other aspects of his thought, is nonetheless an essential aspect of the integrity of his thinking. But before doing so I want to show, by reference to his retrospective reflection on what he owes to the example of Husserl and what to Heidegger, how this politics flows logically from the way he appropriates, modifies, and extends the lessons of his two great philosophical mentors in a single, rational, coherent, and inclusive philosophical vision. Only then will we have arrived at a full picture of the integrity of Jonas's own thought, both in terms of its own logical development in the span of his life and as an achieved system worthy of more attention than it has thus far received. This alone will justify the bold claim for Jonas's exemplary significance as perhaps the preeminent practical thinker for our time with which this book began.

The point here is the Aristotelian point that, just as metaphysics is the supreme expression of man's theoretical reason, articulating his most general understanding of the real, so politics is the preeminent science of practice, through which alone his conditions of survival and well-being can be ensured. Only an ontologically grounded ethics, and hence a metaphysically informed politics, can answer to the needs of the time, and this is what Jonas provides—not, to be sure, in a programmatic system from which sound policy can be mechanically deduced, but pointing to the range of considerations of which future practice must take account.

First, then, the Husserlian dimension developed in Jonas's thought. When, in 1921, the eighteen-year-old Jonas arrived to study philosophy at the University of Freiburg, the "already graying Husserl" was the leading influence he encountered. The essence of the phenomenological method that Husserl taught was that philosophy could achieve the status of a rigorous science only by beginning, not with hypothetical causal explanations, but with pure description of the objects of consciousness. For Husserl himself this program involved abstracting the task of description from all questions of whether or not such objects actually existed and was thus, in principle, metaphysically neutral. This did not stop many of his students from taking it as warranting, as Husserl's own teacher, the Catholic philosopher Brentano had done, an attribution of autonomous metaphysical reality to such objects, and Jonas points to the historical fact that exposure to Husserl's rigorously descriptive method—in which the objective properties of the objects of consciousness, their *noematic* quality, were carefully distinguished from the *noetic* process in which, descriptively, they were revealed—led many of his students toward religion.

Jonas gives the examples of Max Scheler and Edith Stein as two figures in whom exposure to Husserlian method led to their own conversion to a Catholic faith in God as a consequence of the natural theological realism to which acceptance of the autonomous properties of consciously encountered objects seemed to lead. In other cases, notably that of Nicolai Hartmann, a similar process led to the development of a systematic naturalistic realism, empty of religious content, but no less emphatically ontological for that. Both these steps seemed to Husserl philosophically illegitimate by virtue of the fact that, in his view, revelation of the *noematic* properties of the objects of consciousness gave no warrant for judging whether or not such objects actually existed independently of their presence to the consciousness in which they were constituted and revealed. And this, as is well known, led Husserl himself in the direction not of ontological realism but of a transcendental idealism that identified the scientific status of objects as merely the necessary objective correlates of the operation of the transcendental, as opposed to personal, ego. It is not our purpose to expound the reasons that led Husserl to this conclusion, so apparently at variance with what many took to be the realistic implications of his initial descriptive method, beyond noting, with Jonas, that it was paradoxically a function of his determination, against the speculative and hypothetical tenor of nineteenth-century thought, to make philosophy a rigorous, descriptive science of the given contents of consciousness.

Jonas was one of many students of Husserl who learned from him the descriptive method of phenomenology while refusing to follow him along the idealist path. This seemed to him a consequence of Husserl's artificial restriction of the object to being a correlate of pure consciousness alone, without regard to the no less relational status of the body in which consciousness is set. "What about the existence of our *body,* I asked myself. Can we reduce it as well to a 'datum of consciousness' without robbing the datum to be described of its real import—namely, that which is at stake in the existence or nonexistence of the subject itself?" (*MM,* 43).

It was on this doubt that the impact of Heidegger's *Being and Time* operated in showing that the primary place of the conscious ego was the world-engaged being concerned with its own existence, *Dasein.* And yet, as we have seen, even Heidegger's ontology of *Dasein* seemed to Jonas unduly restrictive in isolating its account of human existence from "the testimony of our physical and biological evolution" (*MM,* 48). Heidegger professed, against Husserl's emphasis on pure consciousness, to be concerned with the question of being, ontology: "But instead of taking account of [the] massively material basis that after all propounds the riddle, he invokes as our underlying determinant a highly spiritual entity that he calls *'das Seyn'* (the German word for 'Being' in an archaic spelling). Here again, as previously in his overlooking of the body, this means that the question of Being was spared the tremendous impact of considering the reciprocal relationship of human beings and nature—a relationship which at this very moment was entering a new and critical phase, although this was still unrecognised at the time" (*MM,* 48–49).

The "new and critical phase" to which Jonas refers was the threat to existence, with which the ontology of *Dasein* professes to be concerned. This threat was manifest, first, by the violence unleashed on the world of his personal being by National Socialism, and second, by the impact of global technology of which Heidegger says so much but to whose regulation he provides no rational solution—as steadily, in his later thought, he withdraws from political engagement to a quasi-mystical expectation of a new dispensation of Being. Jonas's ethics of responsibility is his attempt to remedy this practical lacuna in Heidegger's thought, as his philosophy of organic being is his attempt to flesh out the abstractly spiritual quality of an existentialism that fails, first, to acknowledge adequately, if at all, the material bodily base of existential concern in the orientation of the organism to its bodily survival, and then, in the special case of man, to the consequent ethical imperative of ensuring his endurance as a moral being called to decide his own fate.

The philosophy of the organism, the anthropology of the particular organism that is man, and the ethics of responsibility are three successive stages in Jonas's systematic attempt to remedy the theoretical and practical deficiencies of Heidegger's fundamental ontology of *Dasein*—man's situated being in the world. The fourth, I suggest, is his implicit politics of human survival. Unlike his lifelong friend and colleague Hannah Arendt, also a Jewish student of Heidegger, or Leo Strauss for that matter, Jonas was never primarily a political philosopher, but he was a philosopher of politics nonetheless. And, although fragmentary, what he says about the political implications of his ontology and his ethics is an essential aspect of any overall account of his work especially because, in his clear statement of the political dilemmas with which we are likely to be faced in the future, he poses a fundamental problem that our politically permissive and democratic age prefers, understandably enough, to evade. It is on this necessarily uncomfortable note that I shall bring

this book to an end, leaving for a future work of political anthropology the task of developing further the implications for human
practice it seems to suggest.

The word *politics* derives from the Greek term for the city-state,
the *polis*. Consequently, the field of politics as a sphere of activity—
in Aristotelian terms, a practical science—is coextensive with the
sphere of being for which man is institutionally responsible. And
this, in our day, is more extensive than ever before, encompassing
the realm of nature on which his survival depends and now itself de-
pendent on the exercise of his judgment. Let us recall here again
what Jonas says of this in *The Imperative of Responsibility*: "[T]he
boundary between 'city' and 'nature' has been obliterated: the city
of men, once an enclave in the nonhuman world, spreads over the
whole of terrestrial nature and usurps its place. The difference between the artificial and the natural has vanished, the natural is swallowed up in the sphere of the artificial, and at the same time the total artifact . . . generates a 'nature' of its own, that is, a necessity with
which human freedom has to cope in an entirely new sense. . . . Issues never legislated before come into the purview of the laws which
the total city must give itself so that there will be a world for the
generations of man to come" (*IR*, 10). At the same time, the extension of the human capacity to control our own fate, and perhaps,
through genetic manipulation, to modify our nature, engenders new
expectations, not untouched by fear, with which in some ways the
political ethic of liberal democracy, subject as it is to the pressures
of popular demand, finds it difficult to cope. Here, then, is an intrinsic tension with which the politics of the future must inevitably
deal.

When Jonas wrote about these issues in 1985, he pointed to two
areas of potential threat to human existence in which this tension
was manifest. Both are rooted in what he called "modern megatechnology"—a phrase that, given the ontological levels into which technological agency extends, is perhaps of more than propagandistic
import. For what distinguishes the "megatechnology" of modernity
from the characteristic technologies of former times is indeed an ontological distinction resulting from the fact that while previous technologies could bring an end to present lives, modern megatechnology embodies the possibility of ending planetary life as such, and,
short of that, the future endurance of men as moral beings capable

of making ethically informed choices. With the end of the balance of terror of the Cold War in the wake of the collapse of the Soviet Union, the latter is now a more urgent threat than the former but all the more threatening for that because, unlike the threat of global destruction, its furtherance can be the consequence of motivations apparently good in themselves.

Of these, Jonas points especially to the dangers inherent in the genetic modification of our nature and the disturbance of the ecological balance between man and the biosphere on which he depends. It is not hard to imagine how each of these, already present in the capacities of current technology, might be extended for apparently good, humane reasons with consequences catastrophic for human well-being. The well-attested phenomenon of global warming is symptomatic of how far we have already traveled along one such route in pursuit of all too desirable comforts within the more technologically developed parts of the world and that the rest of mankind would understandably like to share. And this is only an external, environmental dimension of a problem that, with the development of the possibilities of biological engineering, is increasingly fraught with implications for the inner form—the essence—of man. Each step along the way can be readily justified as serving a particular sectional interest of mankind, but the results of the whole may be disastrous.

This is why Jonas stresses the need for what, memorably, he calls a "heuristics of fear"—a willingness to educate ourselves to the possibilities of the worst consequences of our best-intended actions and be guided by the fears they engender. If this seems an unbalanced view, we should consider that what it in fact does is merely to counteract the inherently destabilizing results of a politics driven by demand and the innovatory dynamic of a technology whose long-term results no one can foresee.

There is in this consideration nothing remarkable as such. The Western public is used to prognoses of impending ecological disaster and warnings about "playing God" with the genetic composition of man and world. There are, in fact, increasing signs that an undiscriminating overattention to such voices is leading to a growing distrust of technology, science, and even reason itself. Much of so-called New Age literature is imbued with an obscurantist nature mysticism, often adorned with selective borrowings from the sup-

posed greater wisdom of currents of Oriental thought deemed innocent of responsibility for either the gifts or burdens of modernity.
Jonas's, though, is no such voice. His warnings are provisional, not
fatalistic, and the remedies he suggests involve not an abandonment
of Western reason and science, which is neither desirable nor possible, but its extension in a retrieval of the logic of an essentially Aristotelian practical philosophy, novel only in the scope of issues of
which it must now take account.

These considerations hold for his ethics of responsibility in a
technological age and for his political considerations as well. Here,
as he was aware, his reflections are not only intrinsically disturbing
but also susceptible to misinterpretation, touching, as they do, on
the question of the restraints on freedom of scientific research and
political practice that may be necessary if future human survival and
identity is to be assured. For what they raise is, on the one hand, the
inherent limitations of the earthly resources on which we depend,
and, on the other, the vulnerability of our essential humanity to ex-
perimentation that may put it at risk.

The pages in "Toward an Ontological Grounding of an Ethics for
the Future" in which Jonas discusses these issues are among the
most discomforting that he wrote. At the same time, they are among
the most important. They testify to the integrity of a thinking imbued not only with an ethical conviction of the importance of ensuring our future as free and therefore moral beings, capable of
choice—and so made, as Jonas thought, in the image of God—but
also with a calculation of what such a task may *potentially* involve.
I stress *potentially* because it seems to me neither fair to Jonas's memory, nor conducive to our capacity to learn from what he says, to ignore the fact that the "worst-case scenario" that he urges us to consider is based upon trust in the goodness and rationality of what is,
nonetheless, a vulnerable creation and a concomitant recognition of
the fallibility of the human agent in whom its charge is vested. And
in this belief there is nothing gnostic, but only an informed conviction, quasi-religious but not that alone, that there is in us a portion
of the freedom of the God in whose image we are made.

Jonas's discussion of the problem of freedom is both ontological
and political. Indeed, the universal institutional requirement that
individual freedom be in some way and to some extent regulated,
and so constrained, is a simple consequence of man's possession of a

degree of ontological freedom. An unfree being, and a society of automatons, would require no such regulation, for its order would be automatic. But Jonas's focus is not on the problem of human political freedom as such, which, as we have seen, he regards as the anthropologically specific form of the freedom that pertains primordially to animal life as a whole, but on the particular historical position in which the extension of the possibilities of that freedom have reached a point at which human survival may be put at risk. And this the imperative of responsibility—the categorical imperative that governs his ethics—cannot allow. Faced with the choice between freedom and survival, it is survival that must take precedence, not for its own sake, but in order that there may continue to be free human beings in the future. Given this calculation, even "a tyranny would still be better than total ruin"; this Jonas ethically accepts, while noting that such a dire prospect both can and should be averted by enacting at present measures that would only have to be enacted more drastically in the future (*MM,* 111–12).

There is an echo of Hobbes in what Jonas says here, with this distinction: While Hobbes sees the surrender of individual freedom to an absolute sovereign as a perennial necessity entailed by man's tendency to engage in the universally destructive "war of all against all," Jonas regards it as an avoidable possibility, required only by the otherwise uncontrollable potential of a historically specific imbalance between man's agency and the supporting nature on whose survival his own depends. What is for Hobbes an anthropological imperative that he urges us to accept is for Jonas, at most, an ecologically justified possibility—a remedy of last resort—that he warns us to take care to avoid. Therefore, though even tyranny may be preferable to extinction, it is "a worst-case scenario, and it is the foremost task of responsibility at this particular moment in world history to prevent it from happening. This is in fact one of the noblest duties . . . , on the part of the imperative of responsibility to avert future coercion that would lead to lack of freedom by acting freely in the present, thus preserving as much as possible the ability of future generations to assume responsibility. But more than this is involved. At stake is the preservation of Earth's entire miracle of creation, of which our human existence is a part and before which man reverently bows, even without philosophical 'grounding'" (*MM,* 112).

Perhaps here the word *wonder* would better render Jonas's characterization of creation than the more theologically charged *miracle*. Either way, the overtone of cosmic piety, redolent of the worldview of the ancients, is unmistakable. But this is a piety informed both by a calculation of the threat to nature posed by the qualitatively novel extent of potentially disruptive human agency and by a Judeo-Christian recognition of the special position occupied by man as the steward of creation, in whom is vested not just responsibility for its future but a veritable image of its divine creator. Jonas is an ecologically oriented philosopher but not, in Lawrence Vogel's term, a "biotic egalitarian." Our duty to nature is owed not undiscriminatingly for its own sake but primarily for our own; and this sets Jonas apart from the currents of nature mysticism that he sees exemplified in the exponents of the notion of a cosmogonic logos criticized in "Matter, Mind, and Creation" as well as from the fatalism of Heidegger's exaltation of Being at the expense of man, against which his ethical theory is, in part, directed. There is a rationality as well as a focus on freedom of decision in Jonas's reverence toward creation, and this reflects the integrally rational form that shapes his whole recasting of the existential legacy that he inherits from his original mentor and leads him to what I have characterized as his renewal, or retrieval, of the Aristotelian legacy of practical philosophy. This retrieval entails not a resignation of the claims of reason but its extension to encompass the needs, including the political needs, of the time in a rational account of man's enduring finitude and freedom.

I believe it is this that makes Jonas the important figure that I take him to be for an age that requires just such a retrieval if it is to cope adequately with the challenges of a future in which the imperative of human survival can no longer be left either to chance or to the blind dispensations of instrumental technology alone. I do not know of any other figure in twentieth-century thought who has done so much to redeem the claims of philosophy to be considered a still-vital voice in what Michael Oakshott called the "continuing conversation" of mankind, nor one whose considerations range so precisely and extensively over those areas that should concern us most. If this book has done anything to make Jonas's voice more widely heard in the tumult of the times, then that at least of its purpose will have been fulfilled. And more than this the mere commentator cannot hope to do. Whether the times will attend is quite another matter.

Index

Academic disciplines, 35–36, 101
Achilles, 69, 70
Acosmism, 16, 18–20, 22–23, 25, 27
Aeschylus, 68–69
Analogy of being, 51
Analytical philosophy, 47, 63, 133
Ancient nihilism. *See* Nihilism
Animals, 54–55, 56, 67, 73, 86, 107. *See also* Organism
Animate versus inanimate, 42, 52–53, 60–61, 93. *See also* Organism
Anthropological constancy, 11–12, 14, 40, 70–72
Anthropology. *See* Human nature; Philosophical anthropology
Aquinas, Thomas. *See* Thomas Aquinas
Archaeology, 86
Arendt, Hannah, 4, 137
Aristotle and Aristotelianism: on cosmos, 32–33, 41, 58–59; on ethics, 20, 66–67, 88–89; Gnosticism versus, 13; on golden mean, 85–86; Heidegger on, 62; on human nature, 32, 58; Jaeger on, 62; and Jonas generally, 3, 5–6, 13, 25; metaphysics of, 18, 34, 58, 101, 116, 135; and myth, 100; on natural science, 41, 45, 46, 53–54, 57–59, 78, 103; neo-Aristotelianism, 58; on physics, 18, 52–53, 78; on politics, 66, 88, 135, 138; practical philosophy of, 142; on *praxis,* 14–15; on reason, 9, 58; scope of thought of, 37, 142; on soul, 56; on virtue, 85–86
—works: *De Anima,* 58; *Ethics,* 58; *Metaphysics,* 18, 58; *Physics,* 18, 58; *Politics,* 58
Arnold, Matthew, 3, 31, 45
Ars vitae, 68
Art, 74, 96

Astronomy, 31, 53
Atheism, 127
Augustine, St., 1, 4, 111
Auschwitz, 7, 95, 97, 109, 115, 126. *See also* Holocaust

"Back to nature," 86
Balfour, Arthur, 37
Barth, Karl, 100
Being: being-unto-death, 56, 67–68; forgetfulness of Being, 26; Great Chain of Being, 45; Heidegger on, 1, 26–28, 33, 43, 47–48, 56, 66, 80, 105–6, 136–37; and Heidegger's disciples, 134; history of Being, 26, 27, 33, 64, 80, 82, 101; Jonas on Being as a whole, 92; man as "shepherd of Being," 1; Plessner on, 107; rationality and goodness of, 89; Voegelin on, 115
Being and Time (Heidegger), 25, 27, 28, 30, 47–48, 105–6, 111
Being-unto-death, 56, 67–68
Beyond Freedom and Dignity (Skinner), 93
Bible, 51, 69, 70, 108, 110, 111, 116, 121, 128, 130–31
Big Bang, 117, 118, 122
Bioethics, 8, 39, 40, 93–94
Biological engineering, 93–94, 123, 124, 139
Biology: and bioethics, 8, 39, 40, 93–94; biological bedrock of spiritual endeavors, 6; and continuity of all forms of organic being, 54–55; and Creation science, 51–52; definition of philosophical biology, 20, 42; and diverse forms of organic being, 42–43; and evolution, 47, 50–57, 59, 78–79, 90, 91, 113, 116, 119, 123, 124, 125; and evolutionary ethics,

51; and existential determination, 40–41; Jonas's research on, during World War II, 4–5; Jonas's theory of the organism, 4–5, 57–59; and materialism, 50–51, 52; metabolism of organisms, 59–60, 67, 78, 79, 93; nature of scientific research in, 40; and philosophy of life, 46–47, 52–61; Plessner on, 43, 56; professional biologists, 50; and question on life's nature, 46–47; questions on, 39–40; and reductionism, 57; and selfish gene, 51; sociobiology, 50–51; and structural determination, 40–41; Whitehead's philosophy of the organism, 45

Bloch, Ernst, 84

Body, 136, 137. *See also* Human nature

Bosch, Hieronymous, 22

Brain and mind, 46, 48, 72–73, 119

Brave New World (Huxley), 93

Brentano, Franz, 135

Bruns, Gerald, 28

Bultmann, Rudolf: and Christianity, 19, 23, 96–97, 110–11; and Gnosticism, 19, 23, 28, 111; and Heidegger, 110; and Jonas, 3, 6, 18–19, 28, 47, 110–12, 133; and Kant, 97, 112; on metaphysics versus faith, 100, 114

—work: *Primitive Christianity in Its Contemporary Setting,* 19

Canada, 7

Carleton University, 7

Cartesian dualism. *See* Descartes, René; Dualism

Categorical imperative, 88

Catholicism. *See* Roman Catholicism

Chance and Necessity (Monod), 78

"Change and Permanence: On the Possibility of Understanding History" (Jonas), 12, 56–57, 69

Chaos, 17

Chemistry, 46, 117–18, 122–23

Christianity: and Bultmann, 18–19,

23, 96–97, 110–11; and Gnosticism, 13, 19–23, 32; and God as prime mover, 116; and Holocaust, 121, 125, 127; and Jonas's limitations on divine omnipotence, 97, 114, 115, 125; and *memento mori,* 68; and Nicene Creed, 127; and redemptive suffering, 130; and Ricoeur, 128; and soul, 55; and Stoicism, 121; of Thomas Aquinas, 21, 22, 32, 33, 51. *See also* Theology

Cicero, 21, 22, 132

Cloning of humans, 93

Clough, Arthur Hugh, 3

"Concept of God after Auschwitz: A Jewish Voice" (Jonas), 97, 100, 127, 129–31

Consciousness, 72–73, 89, 133, 135–36

Constancy. *See* Anthropological constancy

Continental philosophy, 43, 47

Cooper, David E., 24, 63

Copernicus, 31, 53

Cosmic piety, 15, 20, 21–22

Cosmogonic eros, 117

Cosmogonic logos, 117, 121–22, 124

Cosmologist, 16–17

Cosmos: Aristotle on, 32–33, 41, 58–59; Cicero on, 21; definition of, 16–17, 18, 20–21; endless becoming of, 14; Gnostics' acosmism, 16, 18–20, 22–23, 25, 27; and metaphysics, 18; Pascal on, 31; rational intelligibility of, 16

"Cosmos and the Second Main Principle," 115, 117

Creation science, 51–52

Critical analysis, 43, 57

Critiques (Kant), 39

Cybernetics, 44

Cycles, 118

Darwinism, 47, 50–57, 59, 78–79, 90, 91, 113, 116, 123, 124, 125

Dasein (being-there), 5, 29, 30, 43, 47–

48, 56, 66, 69, 105–6, 107, 119, 120, 136–37. *See also* Being
De Anima (Aristotle), 58
Death. *See* Mortality
Deconstructionism, 63
Deism, 54, 78, 96
De Rerum Natura (Lucretius), 120–21
Descartes, René: on consciousness, 72; and distinction between organism and machine, 60–61; dualism of, 6, 42, 44, 46, 53–56, 59, 79; mechanistic philosophy of, 53–54, 116; and mystery of "ghost in the machine," 53; on nature, 31, 53; on thinking and being, 120; writing style of, 38
Despair. *See* Fatalism
Determinism. *See* Existential determinism; Structural determinism
Dialectical reason, 45
Dialectics of Nature (Engels), 50
Disciplinary boundaries, 35–36, 101
Divine creation. *See* Theology
DNA, 123
"Dover Beach" (Arnold), 3, 31, 45
Dualism, 6, 42, 44, 46, 53–56, 59, 79, 130

Ecology. *See* Environmental issues; Nature
Ecumenic age, 32
Eliot, T. S., 69
Engels, Friederich, 50
Engineering. *See* Biological engineering
Entropy, 67
Entropy of knowledge, 101
Environmental issues, 8, 15, 40, 87–88, 134, 139–42. *See also* Nature
Epicureanism, 120–21
Eternity, 121
Ethics: Aristotle on, 20, 66–67, 88–89; bioethics, 8, 39, 40, 93–94; definition of, 48–49; evolutionary ethics, 51; and heuristics of fear, 86, 139–40; and human reason, 33; Jonas on ethics for technological

age, 1, 5, 8, 9–10, 13, 14, 77–94, 134, 138–42; medical ethics, 8; and metaphysics, 90–91; and nature, 8, 15, 87–89, 134; objectivity of ethical judgment, 12, 13; ontologically grounded ethics, 49, 92–93; and postmodernism, 91; science compared with, 15; traditional ethics, 84
Ethics (Aristotle), 58
Evil, 130. *See also* Holocaust
Evolution, 47, 50–57, 59, 78–79, 90, 91, 113, 116, 119, 123, 124, 125
Evolutionary ethics, 51
Existential determinism, 40–41
Existentialism, 9, 13, 25–33, 42, 57, 62, 70–71, 89, 102, 104, 106, 128, 133
Existential nihilism, 13–14, 18, 23–33, 89, 102

Faith, 96–97, 100, 114, 127–30. *See also* Theology
Fatalism, 9–10, 26–28, 30, 64–66, 82, 102, 142. *See also* Nihilism
Fear, heuristics of, 84–85, 86, 139–40
Feminism, 104
Forgetfulness of Being, 26
Foucault, Michel, 63
Frank, Anne, 126
Frankfurt School of neo-Marxism, 43
Freedom: and divine omnipotence, 130; Hobbes on, 141; and human nature, 61, 91, 130–31, 140–41; Jonas on problem of, 140–41; of the organism, 59–61
Free will, 4, 111
Freiburg University, 105, 111, 135
Fundamental Concepts of Metaphysics (Heidegger), 110

Gadamer, Hans-Georg, 25, 47, 70, 79–80, 105
Gehlen, Arnold, 64, 70
Geisteswissenschaften, 48, 70
Genocide, 126
George, Stefan, 27

German Association for the Blind, 4, 111

Germany: Holocaust in, 7, 95, 97–99, 109, 110, 115, 121, 126–31; Jonas in, 4, 6, 7, 8, 111–12, 125; Nazism in, 4, 7, 27, 37, 79, 80, 105, 111, 137; universities in, 104, 109

Geworfenheit, 30

"Ghost in the machine," 53

Gilson, Étienne, 99, 100

Global warming, 139

Gnosis, 22–23, 29–30, 34

Gnosticism: and acosmism, 16, 18–20, 22–23, 25, 27; compared with Christianity, 13, 19–23, 32; compared with Greek paganism, 18, 20; compared with modernity generally, 6–7, 11–12, 13–14, 26–27, 30, 32; doctrines and myths of, 11; and existentialism, 25–33; existential nihilism of, 13–14, 18, 29–33; Jonas's study on generally, 1, 4, 5, 6, 38, 77, 111; Jonas's terminology of "Gnostic Religion," 12–13; nature of *gnosis,* 22–23, 29–30, 34; Voegelin on, 19, 109

"Gnosticism, Existentialism, and Nihilism" (Jonas), 25–33

Gnostic Religion: The Message of the Alien God and the Beginnings of Christianity (Jonas), 6–7, 11–34

God. *See* Theology

God and Philosophy (Gilson), 99

Golden mean, 85–86

Grace, 22

Great Chain of Being, 45

Greek paganism, 18, 20

Green Party, 8, 86

Gulag, 95

Hartmann, Nicolai, 121, 136

Hector, 69

Hegel, G. W. F., 36, 45, 62, 90, 98, 101, 129–30

Heidegger, Martin: on Aristotle, 62; on Being and *Dasein,* 1, 26–28, 33, 43, 47–48, 56, 66, 80, 105–6, 107, 119, 120, 136–37; and being-unto-death, 56, 67–68; and Cooper, 24; decisionism of, 31; as educator, 2, 3, 4, 24–25, 37, 38, 47, 58, 62, 105, 111, 128, 133, 134; existentialism of, 13, 23–25, 29, 62, 89, 102, 104, 106, 128, 133; fatalism of, 9–10, 26–28, 30, 64–66, 82, 102, 142; *Festschrift* published on eightieth birthday of, 56–57; on "fusion of historical horizons," 70; Gadamer on, 79–80; and hermeneutic philosophers, 47–48; on "hermeneutics of facticity," 49; and historicism, 12; on history of Being, 26, 27, 33, 64, 80, 82, 101; legacy of, as antiscientific irrationalism, 81; and metaphysics, 24, 28, 30; and National Socialism, 27, 79, 80, 105, 111; and philosophical anthropology, 64; on philosophy, 65, 104–5; on Plato, 108; and poetry, 27, 28; on science and technology, 9, 26, 28, 49, 82, 137; significance of, 62–64, 81, 102, 103–5; surveys of, 24; and theology, 44, 108–9; writing style of, 2, 3, 5, 38, 102, 104
—works: *Being and Time,* 25, 27, 28, 30, 47–48, 105–6, 111; *Fundamental Concepts of Metaphysics,* 110; *Question Concerning Technology,* 26, 82

"Heidegger and Theology" (Jonas), 44, 108

Heidegger's Estrangements (Bruns), 28

Helvétius, 50

Hermeneutic philosophy, 47–48

Hermeneutics, 47–49

Hermeneutics of facticity, 49

Herr, David, 82–83

Herz, John, 84

Heuristics of fear, 84–85, 86, 139–40

Heuristics of hope, 85

Hillesum, Etty, 115, 126, 131

Historical skepticism, 71

Historicism, 12

History, 48, 70, 101
History of Being, 26, 27, 33, 64, 80, 82, 101
Hitler, Adolf, 4, 37, 105, 110. *See also* Holocaust; Nazism
Hobbes, Thomas, 141
Hölderlin, Friedrich, 27
Holocaust, 7, 95, 97–99, 109, 110, 115, 121, 126–31. *See also* Nazism
Holocaust in American Memory (Novick), 126–27
Hope, 84–85
Human nature: adaptability of, for survival, 41; and animals, 54–55, 56; Aristotle on, 32, 58; beauty and rationality of, 21; and biological constants, 73–74; and the body, 136, 137; and categorical imperative, 88; and consciousness, 72–73; constancy of, 11–12, 14, 40, 70–72; and cultural products, 74; and freedom, 61, 91, 130–31, 140–41; and hermeneutic philosophy, 48; and language, 74–75, 107–8; and mortality, 56, 67–68, 74, 106; mutability of, 72; and psychological openness, 93; and reason, 90, 91–92; and responsibility, 92–93, 138–42; and technology, 74, 86–87; Thomist comparison of human and divine natures, 21; and universal destruction, 91–92; and vastness and purposelessness of nature, 31; Voegelin on, 115; Von Uexkhull on, 107. *See also* Being; Philosophical anthropology
Hume, David, 14, 38
Husserl, Edmund, 3, 37, 47, 81, 111, 133–36
Huxley, Aldous, 93

Images, 57, 74, 96, 110
"Immortality and the Modern Temper" (Jonas), 44, 91, 100
Imperative of Responsibility: In Search of an Ethics for the Technological Age

(Jonas), 5, 9–10, 13, 26, 40, 44, 77–94, 102, 106, 134, 138
Inanimate. *See* Animate versus inanimate
Information, 118–19, 123
Inorganic and organic compounds, 117–18, 122–23
"Is Faith Still Possible?: Memories of Rudolf Bultmann and Reflections on the Philosophical Aspects of His Work" (Jonas), 110–12
"Is God a Mathematician?" (Jonas), 52, 59–61
Islam, 32, 116
Isolationism, 57
Israel, 7

Jaeger, Werner, 62
Jaspers, Karl, 6
Jeans, Sir James, 44
Jews. *See* Judaism
John, St., 121
Jonas, Hans: academic career of, 7, 77, 132; birth and family background of, 3; in Canada, 7; death of, 132; education of, 3–4, 28, 38, 110–11, 128, 133; emigration from Germany by, 4, 111–12, 125; essay form used by, 43–45, 77; integrity of reflections of, 2–3, 12, 77–78; in Israeli army, 7; as Jewish, 4, 7, 68, 97, 98, 109–10, 114, 127–29; lecture tours by, in later years, 7–8, 82; marriage of, 4, 7; and mother's murder in Auschwitz, 7, 97, 109; and Nazism, 4, 37–38, 79, 109, 126–31, 137; in Palestine, 4, 7; philosophy of, as modern and as recovery and retrieval, 14–15, 46, 120; popularity and reputation of, 7, 8, 80, 82–83, 97; published works by generally, 4, 37, 101–2; return to Germany by, 4, 6; scope of writings by, 3; significance of, 1–3, 9–10, 12, 77, 80–82, 135, 142; as soldier, 4, 5, 7, 8–9, 37–38, 109, 111; in United States, 7,

132; in World War II, 4, 5, 8–9, 37–38, 109, 111; writing style of, 2, 3, 37, 38, 69–70, 82–83, 102
—works: "Biological Engineering," 93–94, 123; "Change and Permanence: On the Possibility of Understanding History," 12, 56–57, 69; "Concept of God after Auschwitz: A Jewish Voice," 97, 100, 127, 129–31; "Gnosticism, Existentialism, and Nihilism," 25–33; *Gnostic Religion: The Message of the Alien God and the Beginnings of Christianity*, 6–7, 11–34; "Heidegger and Theology," 44, 108; "Immortality and the Modern Temper," 44, 91, 100; *Imperative of Responsibility: In Search of an Ethics for the Technological Age*, 5, 9–10, 13, 26, 40, 44, 77–94, 102, 106, 134, 138; "Is Faith Still Possible?: Memories of Rudolf Bultmann and Reflections on the Philosophical Aspects of His Work," 110–12; "Is God a Mathematician?," 52, 59–61; "Life, Death, and the Body in the Theory of Being," 120; "Matter, Mind, and Creation: Cosmological Evidence and Cosmogonic Speculation," 97–98, 100, 102–4, 115–24, 142; "Meaning of Cartesianism for the Theory of Life," 53–54; *Mortality and Morality: A Search for the Good after Auschwitz*, 7, 89, 98–99, 132; "On the Subjects of a Philosophy of Life," 46–47; *Phenomenon of Life: Toward a Philosophical Biology*, 4–5, 39–61, 66; "Philosophical Aspects of Darwinism," 52–53; *Philosophical Essays*, 1, 5, 44, 93–94; "Philosophy at the End of the Century: Retrospect and Prospect," 132–33; "Practical Uses of Theory," 66; "Toward an Ontological Grounding of an Ethics for the Future," 134, 140–42
Judaism: on choosing life, 68; Gnosticism compared with, 32; Hillesum on God, 131; of Jonas, 4, 7, 68, 97, 98, 109–10, 114, 127–29; lack of ultimate authoritative body in, 127–28; and limits of divine agency, 98–99, 114, 121, 125, 130–31; in Middle Ages, 116; and redemptive suffering, 130; and Thirteen Articles of Faith, 127–30

Kant, Immanuel, 5, 6, 10, 20, 39, 58, 88, 97, 112, 114
Kass, Leon, 77
Klages, Ludwig, 86, 117
Knowledge: entropy of, 101; faith versus, 90; growth of, 35–37; limits of, 113
Koestler, Arthur, 53, 127
Kosmos, 17. See also Cosmos

Language, 51, 74–75, 81, 107–8
Law, 76
Lebenswelt (life-world), 81
Leibniz, Gottfried, 55, 95
Life: emergence of, 122–25; Judaism on choosing life, 68; philosophy of, 46–47, 52–61
"Life, Death, and the Body in the Theory of Being" (Jonas), 120
Life-world, 81
Literacy, 35
Logos, 31, 118–19, 121–22, 124
Loot (Orton), 69
Löwith, Karl, 4, 7, 19
Lucretius, 120–21

Maimonides, Moses, 127–30
Malebranche, Nicolas de, 53
Man: His Nature and Place in the World (Gehlen), 64
"Man and History" (Scheler), 64
Manichaean dualism, 130
Marburg University, 4, 28, 110
Marcuse, Herbert, 4
Marx, Karl, 36, 98, 127
Materialism, 50–51, 52

Mathematics, 44
"Matter, Mind, and Creation: Cosmo-
logical Evidence and Cosmogonic
Speculation" (Jonas), 97–98, 100,
102–4, 115–24, 142
Matter versus mind. *See* Dualism
McGill University, 7
"Meaning of Cartesianism for the The-
ory of Life" (Jonas), 53–54
Mechanistic philosophy, 53–55, 116
Medical ethics, 8, 40
Meditation, 100
Megatechnology of modernity, 138–
40. *See also* Science and technology
Memento mori, 56, 67–68
Metabolism, 59–60, 67, 78, 79, 93
Metaphysical philosophy, 43, 91–93,
101
Metaphysics: of Aristotle, 18, 34, 58,
101, 116, 135; and cosmos, 18; and
divine creation, 96; and ethics, 90–
91; and faith, 96–97, 100; and Hei-
degger, 24, 28, 30; and Heidegger's
disciples, 133–34; and human arti-
facts, 74, 96; Jonas's metaphysical
philosophy, 43, 91–93, 101; Leibniz
on, 95; and postmodernism, 47, 91;
and reason, 33–34; role of, 65; and
science, 50–51; and technology, 80;
and theology, 99–101, 114. *See also*
Ontology
Metaphysics (Aristotle), 18, 58
Midgley, Mary, 41
Mind and brain, 46, 48, 72–73, 119
Mind versus matter. *See* Dualism
Mishnah, 127
Modern nihilism. *See* Nihilism
Monod, Jacques, 78
Moral nihilism. *See* Nihilism
Mortality, 56, 67–68, 74, 106
*Mortality and Morality: A Search for
the Good after Auschwitz* (Jonas), 7,
89, 98–99, 132
Moses, 108, 109
Multiculturalism, 104
Murder in the Cathedral (Eliot), 69

Murdoch, Iris, 41
Myth, 100, 114, 118

National Socialism. *See* Nazism
Natural selection, 54, 78–79, 116, 119.
See also Evolution
Nature: "back to nature," 86; bound-
ary between city and, 87, 138;
Descartes on, 31, 53; and ethics, 8,
15, 87–89, 134, 139; and global
warming, 139; Jonas's philosophy
of, 8, 12, 15, 20, 45; nature mysti-
cism, 139–40, 142; renewal of, 15;
Schelling on, 45; scientific manipu-
lation of, 15; and wonder of cre-
ation, 141–42
Nature of the Gods (Cicero), 132
Nazism, 4, 7, 27, 37, 79, 80, 105, 111,
137. *See also* Holocaust
Negative theology, 23
Neo-Aristotelianism, 58
Neo-Kantianism, 104
Neo-Platonism, 23, 45
New Age, 139–40
Newman, John Henry, 36–37
New School for Social Research, 7, 132
New Science of Politics (Voegelin), 19
New Testament. *See* Bible; Christianity
Newton, Sir Isaac, 67, 116
Nietzsche, Friedrich Wilhelm, 31, 64
Nihilism, 13–14, 18, 23–33, 62–64,
65, 78, 79, 89, 95–96, 102. *See also*
Fatalism
Noematic properties, 135, 136
Noetic process, 135
Novick, Michael, 126–27

Oakshott, Michael, 142
Objectivity of ethical judgment, 12, 13
Occasionalism, 53
Old Testament. *See* Bible
"On the Subjects of a Philosophy of
Life" (Jonas), 46–47
Ontology: and anthropology, 57; Carte-
sian mechanistic ontology, 53–55;
definition and role of, 44, 48–49, 65;

and dualism of Descartes, 79; and ethics, 49, 92–93; and freedom of the organism, 61; Heidegger's fundamental ontology of *Dasein*, 56, 66, 106; and problem of freedom, 140–41; reduction of, to questions of physics, 44; and science and technology, 49; of transhistorical human constancy, 70–71. *See also* Metaphysics

Order of being, 116, 119

Order of perception, 116, 119

Oresteia (Aeschylus), 69

Organic and inorganic compounds, 117–18, 122–23

Organism: form of, 60–61; freedom of, 59–61; Jonas's theory of, 4–5, 57–59; and metabolism, 59–60, 67, 78, 79, 93. *See also* Biology

Original sin, 22

Orton, Joe, 69

Paganism, 18, 20

Palestine, 4, 7

Paley, William, 54

Pascal, Blaise, 30–31, 100

Phenomenological description, 43, 57

Phenomenology, 133, 136

Phenomenon of Life: Toward a Philosophical Biology (Jonas), 4–5, 39–61, 66

Philo Judaeus, 19

Philosophical anthropology: basic principle of, 92; and biological constants, 73–74; and cultural products, 74; definition of, 64, 106–7; and evidential proof, 76; Gehlen on, 64, 70; and Heidegger, 64, 104–5; Jonas on, 52, 66, 69–76; and language, 74–75, 107–8; Plessner on, 43, 64, 70; Scheler on, 17, 64, 70, 106–7; as subset of philosophical biology, 57; and theology, 96, 110

"Philosophical Aspects of Darwinism" (Jonas), 52–53

Philosophical biology, 20, 39–61. *See also* Biology

Philosophical Essays (Jonas), 1, 5, 44, 93–94

Philosophy: analytical philosophy, 47, 133; continental philosophy, 43, 47; cross-fertilization between science and, 38; fatalistic philosophy, 9–10, 26–28, 30, 64–66, 82, 102; and the future, 132–42; Heidegger on, 65; hermeneutic philosophy, 47–48; and isolationism, 57; Jonas's philosophy of life, 46–47, 52–61; Jonas's philosophy of nature, 8, 12, 15, 20, 45; Jonas's reflections on, in later life, 132–33; mechanistic philosophy, 53–55, 116; metaphysical philosophy, 91–93; role of, 65, 97, 113; science distinguished from, 48; and theology, 109–10. *See also* specific philosophers

"Philosophy at the End of the Century: Retrospect and Prospect" (Jonas), 132–33

Philosophy of history, 101

Philosophy of physics, 103

Physics, 44, 46, 50, 52–53, 65, 74, 78, 96, 103, 116–17, 119, 122

Physics (Aristotle), 18, 58

Piety, 15, 20, 21–22, 126, 142

"Place of Man in the Cosmos" (Scheler), 17

Plato and Platonism, 25, 68, 100, 108, 109

Plessner, Helmuth, 43, 56, 64, 70, 106, 107

Plotinus, 23

Politics: Aristotle on, 66, 88, 135, 138; Jonas on politics of survival, 134, 137–42; origin of term, 138

Politics (Aristotle), 58

Postmodernism, 24, 63, 66, 91, 102

Pound, Ezra, 30

Practical reason, 6, 9–10, 20, 26, 142

"Practical Uses of Theory" (Jonas), 66

Praxis, 9, 14–15

Precautionary principle, 84

Pre-Socratic philosophers, 103

Primitive Christianity in Its Contemporary Setting (Bultmann), 19
Principle of hope, 84–85
Psychological openness, 93
Psychology, 48

Qualitative continuity principle, 55–56
Question Concerning Technology (Heidegger), 26, 82

Reason: Aristotle on, 9, 58; dialectical reason, 45; and human nature, 90, 91–92; and metaphysics, 33–34; practical reason, 6, 9–10, 20, 26, 142; and theology, 89–90, 95
Reason in the Age of Science (Gadamer), 47
Redemptive suffering, 130
Reductionism, 57
Religion, 125–26. *See also* Christianity; Islam; Judaism; Roman Catholicism; Theology
Res extensa, 59
Resignation. *See* Fatalism
Resolute decision, 5
Responsibility, 1, 5, 8, 9–10, 13, 14, 77–94, 92–93, 134, 138–42
Ricoeur, Paul, 128
Roman Catholicism, 127, 135
Rosenszweig, Franz, 62
Rousseau, Jean-Jacques, 86

Santayana, George, 38
Sartre, Jean-Paul, 71
Scheler, Max, 17, 64, 70, 106–7, 135
Schelling, Friedrich, 36, 45, 101
Scholasticism, 32, 33, 116, 119
Science and technology: Aristotelian science, 41, 45, 46, 53–54, 57–59, 78, 103; and causality, 113–14; and Creation science, 51–52; cross-fertilization between philosophy and, 38; and education of scientists, 50; ethics compared with, 15; Hegel on, 36; Heidegger on, 9, 26, 28, 49, 82,

137; and heuristics of fear, 84–85, 139–40; Jonas on ethics for technological age, 1, 5, 8, 9–10, 13, 14, 77–94, 134, 138–42; manipulation of nature by, 15; megatechnology of modernity, 138–40; and metaphysics, 50–51; nature of scientific research, 40; and ontology, 49; Pascal on, 30–31; philosophy distinguished from, 48; and precautionary principle, 84; professional scientists, 49–50; Schelling on, 36; and technological imperative, 85–86; Voegelin on, 2; Weber on, 62. *See also* Biology; Chemistry; Mathematics; Physics
Scientific Creationism, 51–52
Scruton, Roger, 36
Selfish gene, 51
Situated being, 5
Skepticism, 71, 75–76
Skinner, B. F., 93
Snow, C. P., 35
Social sciences, 48, 70
Sociobiology, 50–51
Sociology, 48
Socrates, 7, 68, 69
Sosein, 30, 107
Soul, 22, 55, 56, 73
Specialization, 35–36
Spinoza, Baruch, 55, 127
Stages of Organic Life and Man (Plessner), 43, 56, 64
Stein, Edith, 126, 135
Steiner, George, 24, 36, 102
Stoicism, 21, 22, 68, 121
Strauss, Leo, 4, 62, 63–64, 70, 81, 102, 105
Structural determinism, 40–41
Subjectivity, 124
Suffering, 130
Symbols, 73, 75

Techne, 9
Technological age, 86–87. *See also* Science and technology
Teilhad de Chardin, Pierre, 42, 98

Teleology, 31, 45, 67, 78

Thales, 103

Theology: and Bultmann, 96–97; and challenge of nihilism, 95–96; and Creation science, 51–52; and Deism, 54, 78, 96; and divine creation, 91, 95–97, 108–9, 114–16, 119–20, 124–25, 130–31; and Heidegger, 44, 108–9; and Holocaust, 97–99, 100, 126–31; Jonas on, as "luxury of reason," 95, 97, 99, 114; Jonas's lecturing on, 7; Jonas's rejection of divine omnipotence, 97, 114, 115, 125, 130–31; Jonas's writing style on, 2–3, 102; knowledge versus faith, 90; and life's emergence, 122–25; and man's freedom, 91; and metaphysics, 99–101, 114; in Middle Ages, 95; and philosophical anthropology, 96, 110; and philosophy, 109–10; and physical structure of universe, 121–22; and reason, 89–90, 95; and supernatural divine intervention in causal order of world, 112–14; and Thales, 103. See also Christianity; Gnosticism; and specific theologians

Theory, 66

Thermodynamics, second law of, 123

Thirteen Articles of Faith (Maimonides), 127–30

Thomas Aquinas, 21, 22, 32, 33, 51

Tomb, 57, 74, 96, 110. See also Mortality

Tools, 57, 74, 86, 96, 110

Torah, 127, 128

"Toward an Ontological Grounding of an Ethics for the Future" (Jonas), 134, 140–42

Trakl, Georg, 27

Transcendence, 42

Truth and Method (Gadamer), 47, 70

Umwelt (environment of animals), 107

Understanding, 73

Universe. See Cosmos

Universities, 35–37, 101, 104, 109

Virtue, 85–86

Voegelin, Eric, 2, 19–20, 32, 33, 75, 100–101, 109, 115

Vogel, Lawrence, 7, 89, 90, 91, 95–96, 142

Von Uexkhull, Jacob, 107

Warnock, Mary, 41

Weaver, Richard, 65

Weber, Max, 62

Welt (world of man), 17, 107

Whitehead, Alfred North, 45

Wittgenstein, Ludwig, 38, 47, 80, 81

Wolpert, Lewis, 51

World. See Cosmos

World War II, 4, 5, 8–9, 37–38, 109, 111

Zoroastrianism, 32